"Protesting the typical and simplistic messages that reduce information about the Middle East to quick political slogans or eschatological schemes, Murray cries out persuasively that our evangelical agenda often abandons or minimizes the gospel message. Murray calls us back to the person of Jesus and the message of His death and resurrection, pleading with us to restore its centrality, contrary to the periphery discussions that not only detract from the gospel but actually offend the very folks we most want to reach. We need to hear and heed Murray's timely warning."

—GARY R. HABERMAS
Distinguished Research Professor
Liberty University
Lynchburg, VA

"This book by former Muslim Abdu Murray provides a perspective that is level-headed, insightful, and caring. Murray is well acquainted with the mind-set shared by many Muslims and Jews in both the Middle East and North America. This book is a valuable contribution for Christians, informing them that they are talking past Muslims and Jews, and how to turn that around."

—MICHAEL LICONA
Apologetics Coordinator
North American Mission Board
Atlanta, GA

"Written from the illun   ristian
who grew up in a Leba_____ay pres-
ents a genuinely biblical and more fruitful alternative in response to the strife, suffering, and injustices the Middle

East region has endured. Murray proposes a bold—and far more promising—way forward."

—PAUL COPAN
Professor and Pledger Family Chair of
Philosophy and Ethics
Palm Beach Atlantic University
West Palm Beach, FL

"Thought-provoking insights from the Scriptures colored by the unique background and qualifications of the author."

—NABEEL T. JABBOUR
Professor and Author
Colorado Springs, CO

APOCALYPSE LATER

Why the Gospel of PEACE
Must Trump the POLITICS of PROPHECY
in the MIDDLE EAST

Abdu H. Murray

Kregel
Publications

*To my wife and children.
You will never know how much
peace I have because God has
blessed my life through you.*

CONTENTS

ACKNOWLEDGMENTS

This book was completed only because sincere, loving, and committed people helped me along the way. Without their sacrifices of time and effort, I would not have been able to complete even half of the work that has gone into the book now in your hands.

The first person I must thank is my wife, Nicole, who sacrificed so much so that I could pursue the calling that God had given me. She sacrificed time with me, expended untold energy in taking care of our children while I researched and wrote, and took time to review the manuscript and give me valuable insights. She typed, she hole-punched, and she gave of herself all without complaint. Her efforts kept me going even in the most stressful times. She truly exemplified Christ in those times and anchored me with the peace that this book is all about.

My dearest and closest friend, Mickey, spent many hours reviewing chapters and providing comments. His uncanny insights into the Scriptures helped steer me theologically and practically. He was a never-ending source of encouragement.

Brian Wassom, Mike Kern, and Scott Cherry, all of whom have been involved in my ministry, also provided valuable insights. Brian, who is a gifted writer himself, provided much-needed stylistic critiques. Mike, with his penchant for cutting to the chase, gave me practical advice. And Scott, with his (sometimes) brutal honesty, helped me to be real when the temptation to be too lofty was great.

My thanks also go out to Michael Licona, the apologetics coordinator for the North American Missions Board. Mike was instrumental in encouraging me to write and getting me in touch with Kregel Publications.

I would be remiss if I did not thank the many others who, at one time or another, provided guidance and insight. To all the other board members of Aletheia International not previously mentioned: Steve Norman, Tony Rea, Jack Aliotta, and Bruce Rubin, you have my most sincere thanks. My father-in-law, Jan, and my mother-in-law, Sandy, were always encouraging. Paradoxically, I must also thank my father, mother, and extended family. Without all of the love and support they gave me growing up and in my adult life, I would not have come to the place that I have. Though we may have our religious differences, they are always on my mind and in my heart.

Finally and most importantly, I must thank God. At times, the strength He provided me was the only thing that sustained me during this project. This work is all about Him and His power to sustain us all in these trying times.

INTRODUCTION

If this life has one defining characteristic, it is the universal presence of conflict. Some places in the world have more than their share of conflict, while others suffer through it to a much lesser degree. When we think of major world conflicts, probably the Middle East is the first to pop into our minds. I venture to say that the words *Middle East* seldom appear in print or are heard over the airwaves without the word *conflict* immediately following. In fact, we have capitalized the word *conflict* in the phrase, so that now we discuss the "Middle East Conflict."

The Middle East Conflict is incredibly, almost impossibly, complex. There are racial/ethnic issues. There are land entitlement issues. There are poverty issues. Indeed, the conflict does not involve just Israel and Palestine. It has evolved into conflicts among Israel, Syria, Egypt, Jordan, Iraq, and Lebanon. The complexities have spilled over to countries in Africa and Asia. Iran, Pakistan, and Afghanistan are all implicated in the Middle East Conflict, though none of them is an Arab country. The complexities have even crossed oceans, involving the United States and South American countries. Many, many people have tried their hand at solving the problems among these nations. Books on the geopolitical theories and the political science of the Middle East Conflict and other world conflicts abound. Any reader interested in discovering theories about the causes of and solutions to the conflict from every side has an unlimited supply of material to satisfy himself or herself. It seems that the mire of the conflict's complexity makes the solutions that have been offered untenable. But the struggle to find political and social solutions to conflicts, especially the Middle East Conflict, persists. And indeed it should.

But what has been overlooked in this struggle is the presence of simplicity in conflict. All conflicts share at least two things in common. First, all conflicts have a fundamental cause that is spiritual in nature, although more worldly issues have eclipsed that spiritual cause. Second, all conflicts lead those who are affected by them to ask deep, fundamental questions about the nature of conflict and how it fits into ultimate purpose. This is true of those who are in the middle of the conflict as well as those whose homeland or relatives are in the thick of the strife, even though they themselves may be thousands of miles away. Often, the issues are complex and deal with border disputes, resources, and self-governance. But what is more interesting and important to see is that the tangible aspects of conflict— the loss of life, property, and rights—lead those affected by it to ask profound questions about the intangible aspects of life and purpose. Thus, like the fundamental cause of conflict, the fundamental questions that arise from conflict are spiritual. It is how the fundamental cause is addressed and the fundamental questions are answered that lead to either more conflict or the spread of peace.

While the rest of the world seems to have ignored these fundamental causes and questions, the evangelical church in the West has at least given them some kind of attention. The Western church has been churning out a growing number of "spiritual-historical" books on conflict, especially the Middle East Conflict. Such books tend to trace the millennia-old religious and spiritual causes of the enmity between the Jews, the sons of Isaac, and the Arabs, the sons of Ishmael. But most of those fine efforts have tended to focus on incendiary, hot-button issues: Zionism, Christian Zionism, and eschatology, the so-called end times. With this focus, the church has basically made the Middle East Conflict the crucible for its in-house debate on those issues. While those issues are important to debate within Christianity, the church has been making that debate the primary message it sends to the non-Christian world. Ironically, the church has attempted to address the fundamental issues of the conflict with the peripheral issues of Christianity.

This book is an attempt to shift the focus—especially the church's focus—back to the fundamental answer to the fundamental questions. That fundamental answer is the gospel. In the early chapters, I call out to the body of believers in Christ to change what it has been shouting to the non-Christian world, because what it has been shouting, and the manner in which it has been shouting it, has kept non-Christians away from the gospel. In the later chapters, I show how only the Christian worldview answers the fundamental questions that rise up from the ashes of conflict and provides true peace. More to the point, I endeavor to show that the answers are not really found in an "-ism" or an "-ology," as such, but in a person, the very person of Jesus Christ.

It may seem audacious, arrogant, or simplistic to claim to offer a single solution for the Middle East Conflict and every other conflict. Indeed it *would* be, if I were suggesting a one-size-fits-all solution to the complex political and social issues that come with conflict. But I am not. What I am suggesting may still be audacious but in a different sense. I am making the rather unpopular claim that there is only one answer to the fundamental questions that arise from conflict, and that answer is the gospel. I claim that if the fundamental issues are answered on a spiritual level, then the superficial issues will come into sharper focus, the players in the conflict will have better understanding, and the efforts toward lasting political solutions will be more fruitful.

In writing this book, I have tried very hard to avoid a few things. I have tried to avoid critiquing or championing any one eschatological viewpoint. (I actually think that many of the differing eschatological views within Christian orthodoxy have valid points, but they all have their problems as well.) I have avoided trying to offer a political solution to the Middle East Conflict. Quite frankly, people far more qualified than I have tried their hand at that. In writing this book, I have tried hardest to avoid being overly simplistic. We have seen many bumper stickers providing such sentiments as, "No Jesus, No Peace; Know Jesus, Know Peace." In some ways, that is the basic message of this book, and I believe it. But the world is looking for more substance. I have tried very hard to make the message simple, but not as simplistic as a bumper sticker. Additionally, while most readers of this book will be Christians, it is my prayer that this is a conversation that non-Christians can listen in on.

I am not saying that if we all believe the same thing, then there will be peace. If current events teach us anything, it is that a society that fervently believes together does not necessarily stay together. The millions of Muslims in Iraq all believe the same fundamentals about their religion, but that country has experienced chaos at least in part because people who cling to the same fundamental theology have been killing each other. African-American Christians and white American Christians all claim to hold to the same basic theology, yet the history of race relations in America gives the lie to the notion that agreement of belief equates to peace. Thus, I cannot even argue that if we all just believed in Christianity, we would have peace.

The message I am trying to espouse is this. The gospel informs us about what conflict really is, and it informs us about what peace really is. The gospel informs us of what it means to have peace despite conflict—and even because of it. It is when the church begins spreading that gospel message, and when more and more people come to fully understand its implications, that we will begin to achieve earthly peace. Perhaps there is only a small difference between that argument and the simplistic argument that if we all just believe in Jesus, we will all get along. But it is my prayer that as you read these pages you will see that this little difference makes all the difference in the world.

Chapter 1

SORROW, JUSTICE, AND LOVE

Conflict Within

I was greeted by two seemingly conflicting sets of sounds as I walked into my parents' suburban Detroit home one sunny day in May of 2000. One set of sounds came from my parents and brothers. They were jubilant and celebratory. The other sounds came from my parents' television set and were the distinctive sounds of the Arabic news broadcasts from various Middle Eastern satellite networks. I found the two sets of sounds to be conflicting because Middle Eastern news broadcasts (far more even than those from America) seldom give good or happy news. Growing up with Arabic stations on the television, I had come to associate Middle Eastern news broadcasts with doom and gloom. Yet on this occasion, my parents were practically giddy.

Curious, I rushed into the family room to find my parents, especially my father, animated and celebrating. He alternated from sitting on the edge of his favorite armchair to standing or pacing about. With remote control in hand, he was frantically changing channels between the local news stations and the international satellite broadcasts. On every channel we saw the images of Lebanese people, both in Lebanon and in the nearby city of Dearborn, Michigan, flooding the streets, holding up Lebanese flags, and cheering.

Although the broadcasts made readily apparent what was happening, my father said to me in a joyous tone, "Israel is finally pulling out of South Lebanon!"

The jubilation, of course, stemmed from the fact that my family is of Lebanese, Shi'a (called "Shi-ite" in the West) Muslim descent. Most of us hail from a midsized village in south-central Lebanon. It is a predominantly Shi'a village, and my family was and is a large part of it. For many years, Lebanon, especially south Lebanon, had been the staging ground for attacks by the Palestinian Liberation Organization (PLO) against Israeli military and civilian targets, after it had been forced out of the Palestinian territories. Israel responded with devastating attacks on Lebanon, aimed at eliminating the PLO. Those attacks left many Lebanese civilians homeless, childless, parentless, limbless, and lifeless. Sadly, the general populace of Lebanon became caught in the crossfire of a raging conflict in which the Lebanese usually suffered more casualties than the actual combatants. Eventually, Israel occupied a large part of south Lebanon in an attempt to control the threat to its security. Many Muslim Lebanese were outraged at the attacks and the occupation. To combat the occupation, the militant group Hezbollah (which means "Party of God") was formed. This group, made up of volunteer fighters from various villages in Lebanon, launched its attacks against Israeli positions in Lebanon and just across the northern border of Israel. At the same time, Lebanon was suffering through a horrible, fifteen-year civil war between rival factions and militias. After the end of the Lebanese civil war in the early 1990s, Hezbollah emerged as a popular and influential group among most Shi'a Lebanese and even among some Christian Lebanese.

As the news blared on my parents' television set, we discussed the momentous event briefly. Then my father excitedly said that he was going to Dearborn with some family members to join in the celebration. With the exception of my recent graduation from law school, my father had not been so excited and proud in several years. Within moments he was off to join in the celebrations that lasted not just hours, but days.

Through all of my family's actions that day, I perceived a sense of certainty and hope in a changing future for the Middle East. It was as if a great victory had been achieved, not just by Lebanese, but by all Shi'a Muslims in the world. Israel, supported these many years by the United States, had finally decided to withdraw from Lebanon after having suffered losses for so long at the hands of Hezbollah. Israel's withdrawal meant vindication, not just for Lebanon's national struggle, but also for the Muslims' religious struggle. For Muslims around the world, Israel's occupation of Lebanon (and its control of other territories such as the Golan Heights and the West Bank) was not just a political matter but also an intensely spiritual one. Israel's creation was supported and in part even driven by Western Europe and America. Within those supporting nations, evangelical Christians had been among the most vocal and active supporters. Israel's military campaigns and defensive battles were backed by the West and thus, in the eyes of most Muslims, by Christians. The Southern Lebanese Army, which was allied with Israel during its occupation of Lebanon, was largely made up of those who called themselves Christians. Thus, Lebanon's conflict with Israel was many things. It was Lebanon versus Israel. It was Lebanon versus Lebanon. It was the Jews and the West versus the Arabs. But, more pointedly, it was Christianity versus Islam.

Israel's withdrawal had another effect that proved to be deeply profound over time. And that effect was the affirmation in the minds of Shi'a Muslims that God was on their side. In Islam there are many sects, but the two main sects are Sunni Islam which is the vast majority, and Shi'a Islam. The differences in these two sects are both political and theological. To summarize the differences here is to oversimplify them. Suffice it to say, however, that the differences began during the earliest years of Islam. After Muhammad's death, two groups of Muslims disagreed sharply over who should succeed him as the leader of the Islamic community, or *khalifa*. One group, which became the Sunnis, thought the successor should be an elder follower named Abu Bakr, whom they believe Muhammad had appointed. The other group, which became the Shi'a, believed that the leadership should stay with the "rightly guided" *Ahl-ul Beit*, or family of the prophet. In particular, the Shi'a believed that Ali ibn Abi-Talib, Muhammad's cousin and son-in-law, should lead the community after Muhammad's death. Ultimately, the Sunni view prevailed among the majority, and Abu Bakr was named the first *khalifa*. Since that early dispute, the disagreements between Sunni and Shi'a have ebbed and flowed in their intensity. One thing that has remained constant, however, is a mutual distrust that in recent years has led to quite hateful violence, as the recent situation in Iraq demonstrates. Indeed, although certainly not universally true, many Sunni Muslims, especially in the Gulf countries, look on Shi'a Muslims with disdain. Among the strongest commonalities between Shi'a and Sunni Muslims today, however, is their shared opinion that Israel, with the help of the United States, has illegally occupied Muslim/Arab lands, including Palestine, parts of Syria and Jordan, and South Lebanon.

In light of the tensions between the Sunni majority and the Shi'a minority, Israel's withdrawal was intensely profound within the Islamic community. An ill-equipped, small group of Shi'a Muslim villagers in one of the smallest and militarily weakest Arab countries had beaten one of the most powerful military machines in the world. For the Shi'a, this meant a divine vindication of their cause. God was on their side, as it were, and this would help to legitimize Shi-ism in the Muslim world. Shi'a would no longer stand for being made to feel like second-class citizens in the Muslim community. They had done what Sunni Muslims had failed to do over the past decades— defeat Israel and the West. And the result was the filling of the streets, in America and abroad, with Arabs and Muslims of every stripe and creed. They were jubilant, they were happy, and they were more hopeful about their future than ever.

But as I stood in my parents' family room, I was filled with profound uncertainty and inner conflict. On the one hand, I was happy that the occupation was ending. On the other hand, my feelings were so dissonant within me and with the atmosphere in the room that they were practically disorienting. For most of my life, I had been a proud Muslim who was dedicated to spreading Islam's teachings to anyone who would listen. My parents strongly encouraged my brothers and me to learn about Islam, embrace it, and share it. I had taken that encouragement to heart and learned all I could about the religion of my father and forefathers. But at that moment, when everyone in my close-knit family was rejoicing over the newly brightened futures of Lebanon, Shi'a Muslims, and Arabs, I was struggling with the more fundamental issue of whether Islam could even provide the answers to life's deepest questions.

During the past nine years, I had been engaged in an intense personal investigation of the evidence for the major worldviews. I had studied the tenets of many religious (and nonreligious) systems, but Islam and Christianity held my focus because they seemed to be the most credible. But these two gigantic faiths stood diametrically opposed on some key issues. As the evidence for the historic Christian faith mounted, my unease with my place in my family and my community increased. I often wondered what a decision for Christ would entail for all of us. What consequences would result from such a religious rift? In some ways, I was still a Muslim at that time, and it would be more than a month before I would make a definitive decision to follow Jesus. But during the furor and craze of that day in May 2000, when decades of conflict seemed to be ending, I was profoundly conflicted by all that was happening around me.

My inner conflict had many prongs to it, but the May 2000 "victory over Israel" sharpened the point of one particular prong. As I was discovering the core of the gospel message and the historical evidence for it, I encountered the rather intense debate among evangelicals over eschatology, or the end times as it is popularly referred to. A prevailing view in modern, Western Christianity is dispensationalism. Dispensationalism is a school of biblical interpretation made popular in the nineteenth century by John Nelson Darby, a prominent leader of the Plymouth Brethren in the United Kingdom. Dispensationalism is a rich and complex theological view. But one if it's central features is the view that the biblical entities referred to as the "Church" and "Israel" are two separate entities with two distinct and separate roles to play in the end times, both before and after Armageddon. In the popular culture, dispensationalism is identified largely with those Christians who believe that many, if not most, of the prophecies of the Old Testament and the New Testament have yet to be fulfilled. Vocal dispensationalists believe that these prophecies are being fulfilled before our very eyes in the Middle East.[1] Indeed, some dispensationalists, usually termed Christian Zionists, believe that the creation of the State of Israel in 1948 is the modern-day fulfillment of biblical prophecy.

In 1999, just a few months before Israel's withdrawal from Lebanon, the "Y2K bug" became the world's obsession and the fuel for some Christians' fiery, end-of-the-world prognostications. In that climate, it seemed that the Christian community I was investigating could talk about nothing but the end of the world, how the impending Y2K disaster would usher the Antichrist into power, and how events in the Middle East were fulfilling prophecy. I was hearing over and over again that the Bible teaches that Israel must be established, the Arabs have no right to the Holy Land, that the temple of Solomon must be rebuilt, and the Muslim Dome of the Rock (where the temple once stood) must be destroyed for Jesus to return. At the extreme end of this view, pundits told me and the rest of the Arabs that to allow Arabs any part of the Holy Land would be tantamount to opposing God's people, God's plan, and even God Himself.

January 1, 2000, came and went without incident. Yet, the furor over the end times did not pass. Even as innocent Jews and innocent Arabs died or lost their homes, some Christians were broadcasting that prophecy was being fulfilled. Nearly every time I would find something remarkable that verified the historic Christian faith, I would hear from prominent Christians that Israel is a special nation, a chosen nation, and that Christ would have each of us defend her and support her no matter what. I had no problem with supporting Israel's right to exist or decrying an injustice when she had suffered wrongs. But because I had heard of and seen some of the atrocities and injustices that Israel herself had worked on Palestinians and Arabs, I could not put to rest the paradox of a gospel of love and the message of unquestioning support I was hearing. During my investigation of the evidence for the gospel, my intellectual objections were being resolved, but the powerful emotional barriers remained. More to the point, Christians were actually fortifying my barriers.

Those emotional barriers were the same barriers that nearly every Muslim faces when confronted with the gospel. There are many such barriers, but I daresay that the reaction to statements of ethnic or spiritual inferiority to another group is one of the most dominant. Over and over again, Arabs, especially Muslims, are told that if they are at odds with Israel, they are at odds with God and, that by virtue of being non-Jews, their interests are subordinate to the interests of Israel and Jews. To a people who are characterized by a strong sense of tradition and ethnic importance, there is perhaps no higher and stronger wall that could be erected between Muslims and the gospel.

This kind of wall is similar to the understandable emotional barriers Jews felt when the medieval church labeled them second-class citizens because of their heritage and tried to force them to convert to Christianity. The irony is that the church's treatment of Jews sowed the seeds for the Zionist movement in Europe and later America, the extreme form of which has now resulted in another group, the Arabs, feeling like second-class citizens, undeserving of the same access to justice and fairness as those of a different ethnic or spiritual background. Today, the result has become a never-ending cycle of cruelty and violence wrought by Arabs and Jews against each other, sprinkled only occasionally with a peaceful gesture.

Perhaps the most profound irony, however, is that the most vocal proponents of the idea that one group of people is spiritually superior to another is the mainstream culture of the Western Christian church. In recent years, dispensationalism's end-times message, as characterized by Christian Zionists, has become the central vehicle for this message. For many centuries, however, a countervailing school of biblical interpretation, commonly referred to as covenant theology, has persisted. It, too, was used and abused to set up one group of people to be inferior to another. For some proponents of this view, "Israel" has been replaced by the Christian church since Jesus' first coming and the Jews' rejection of Him as their Messiah. The popular way covenant theology is caricatured, termed by some as "replacement theology," dictates that Jews no longer have any place in God's redemptive plan for mankind and that the church has replaced (or superseded) national Israel as God's people. So it is no surprise that Jews who investigate the credibility of the gospel and come across this view feel repelled when they learn that, by virtue of their heritage, they have been excluded from God's promises.

And so the debate between these views, especially between Christian Zionism and replacement theology regarding the issue of which ethnic group is entitled to the Holy Land, has raged on. I quite vividly recall being bombarded with rhetoric from both sides of the debate. But in the West, most of the rhetoric was from Christian Zionists in the dispensationalist camp. Often I had heard the message that it was the Christian's duty to unconditionally support Israel and condemn her enemies. I could not reconcile such a message with the gospel I was learning about. More to the point, I could not reconcile the implication that Palestinians (and by extension all Arabs) were not entitled to certain property or worthy of support simply by nature of their ethnicity. The lesson for me was not that Israel should be blessed but that Arabs should be denigrated.

It is quite understandable, then, that as a young Arab Muslim I would feel that if Christianity held to such a view, then it was not for me. It is also quite understandable that a Jew, having been told that he is now an outsider, is repelled by what he perceives to be Christianity.

Standing there in my parents' family room in the midst of all the celebration, I battled within myself. I was finding the evidence for the gospel compelling and was on the verge of committing myself to Jesus. But I could not shake the feeling that following Him would mean turning my back on Arabs, Muslims, and my family. How could I do such a thing? In a very real sense, that would be tantamount to suicide of identity. At that moment, I could not decide if I should be happy about Israel's withdrawal from my ancestral homeland or if I should be incensed because "God's Chosen" had been defeated.

My spiritual quest had started out as a quest for truth supported by evidence. I had found that evidence and was drawn to Jesus by that evidence, but now I had to resolve more issues than I was prepared to deal with. My journey had transformed into something more complex than just looking at the evidence. During the years of my study of Islam and Christianity, I had always known that giving my life to Jesus would result in great family upheaval. But as I was confronted with competing eschatological claims, as my family and I were getting the message from Christians that justice for Arabs is subordinate to Jewish interests, I realized that committing to Christ would have deep and lasting implications for me and my family. That day in May of 2000, I was frustrated because the last thing I needed was another emotional barrier with which to deal. So I hid my frustration and gave myself over to the joyous sounds that filled my parents' home. Fearing that I may never have another celebration like this with my family again, I resigned myself to celebrate with them over what appeared to be Lebanon's certain and bright future.

Sorrow, Justice, Love, and the Gospel

How different was the atmosphere among the Lebanese during the war between Israel and Lebanon just six years later in the summer of 2006. Walking into my parents' home during those months was quite a different experience than in May 2000. The television broadcasts no longer showed jubilant Lebanese in the streets. It was back to business as usual. Images of women weeping, men looking frantically for their children, and bodies lying in the streets were prominent and dominant. Ruined buildings in a once sprawling metropolis flooded the screen. The television did not spare us the images of distraught Israelis who also were scrambling through the streets, yelling and screaming to find their loved ones after rocket attacks.

By then I had been a Christian for six years. Space does not permit a full disclosure of my journey to faith, but it suffices to say that the family turmoil I feared had come, but with the Lord's help, we were working out the issues we faced. Having come to faith, one would think that I would be absolutely clear in my thinking about the Middle East situation politically. One would think that I would not find myself in the kind of struggle I faced in May 2000. But I was quite conflicted about the war in 2006. I was conflicted because my faith demanded critical thinking, not blind allegiance to one side or the other. I could not side with Arabs simply because we share DNA, and I could not side with Israel simply because the loudest voices in the church told me to.

But what was crystal clear to me was that leading evangelicals' preoccupation with using the continuous tragedies in the Middle East to put details to their end-times theories was pushing more and more Arabs, Muslims, and Jews away from Christ rather than attracting them. The cries of both Arabs and Jews were practically deafening, but the church was not listening because it was too busy shouting about Armageddon. The Christian church has been so preoccupied with discussing "prophecy," the "end times," and being "left behind" that it has left behind its central concern, which is the spreading of the gospel. Surely, eschatology should be explored and discussed within the church because it is an important part of the Bible. But it has been transformed from an in-house debate to the most prominent message the church is sending to the non-Christian world.

The primacy and impact of this end-times message is well illustrated by an editorial published in *Christianity Today* during the 2006 war between Lebanon and Israel. In that editorial, Martin Accad, a Lebanese Christian and the academic dean of the Arab Baptist Theological Seminary in Lebanon, could no longer hide his frustration over what he perceived to be the church's blindness and myopic views. Railing against Hezbollah, Israel, and America, and especially his fellow evangelicals, Accad poured out the sentiments felt so sharply by so many of Middle Eastern and even Jewish descent. Although I do not necessarily agree with everything Accad wrote in his piece, I quote him extensively here because of the emotion and sweeping range of his words.

> But how is it that [some Christians fail] to notice that world events in the last few years—even decades—have had as their main catalyst tens of thousands of evangelical Christians with a "messianic" mentality who believe that apocalyptic destruction of all but their beloved Israel will be "a precursor to global salvation?" . . .
>
> I'll tell you, if you care, what I think those [neutral governments] will help foster. I think that some pseudo-biblically motivated Christians with decision power, who believe "that apocalyptic destruction is a precursor to global salvation," are presently working toward providing a Middle Eastern conflict of regional significance in order finally to settle accounts with Hezbollah-and-Hamas-supporting Syria, Iran, Lebanon, and Palestine, who have committed the crime . . . of making their hatred for Israel

"crystal clear." And how dare they, since the said state has only been acting as an aggressor and racist colonial state with neighbor-exterminating tendencies from the moment of its inception? . . .

As an academic with a Ph.D. from Oxford University and specialist in Christian-Muslim and East-West relations, constantly seeking creative models of conflict resolution and better understanding, all of what I have just written is written in a manner far from what I would normally write or say with a cool head, from what my Swiss-blood-flowing veins would normally permit me to utter. But then, perhaps academics sometimes owe their readers more genuine feelings, skin-level emotions gushing out of a deeply hurting, frustrated, desperate, and hopeless soul that has had enough of human arrogance and injustice. . . .

I am angry at self-centered Hezbollah, which has done the inadmissible of taking a unilateral war decision without consulting the Lebanese government of which it is part, for never giving a second thought to the hundreds (perhaps thousands) of Lebanese who will perish as a result of its selfish decision. I am angry that citizens of a nation like Israel, who have so suffered at the hands of others, would allow themselves such an out-of-proportion reaction, oh-so-far from the "eye-for-an-eye and tooth-for-a-tooth" principle that we might have forgiven them. I am just as angry at—I have lost hope in—the international community that is keeping silent and not even budging with an official condemnation of this senseless instinct of extermination. By both sides, I would be lynched for what I have just said, if they had the chance. But what have I got to lose anymore?[2]

Whether Accad's political assessments are right or wrong, his urgent emotional sentiments cannot be ignored. Indeed, Accad's sentiments toward the church are especially telling, given that he is neither a Jew nor a Muslim. He is a committed Christian who has actually listened to the cries of the non-Christians suffering in the midst of conflict. From his comments, we can see that the cries of both Arabs and Jews center around three main issues that arise in most conflicts. Those issues are the cry of sorrow, the demand for justice, and the need for love.

First is the cry of intense sorrow. Daily, the news informs us of tragedies that lead to sorrow in every corner of the earth. But the Middle East crisis shows us particularly intense and graphic depictions of the cry of sorrow. In the midst of the 2006 war, the southern Lebanese village of Qana was heavily bombarded because Israel suspected that it was a key Hezbollah stronghold. As the dust cleared, the world was shocked to find out that dozens of children, hiding from the destruction around them, were actually in the center of the maelstrom. Many of those children lost their lives that day just as many children in the same village had in a 1996 shelling. In other bombings, whole families were wiped out with no one left to carry on the family name. At the same time and with just as loud a voice, we hear the cries of families of innocent Israeli Jewish children who lost their lives in rocket attacks and suicide bombings in the public square. In his editorial, Accad echoes the sorrowful cries of those suffering on both sides when he calls himself a "deeply hurting, frustrated, desperate, and hopeless soul." Ironically, these two cultures in combat have manufactured a startling common thread between them: the desire to know if their tragedies, if their sorrows, have any ultimate purpose. It is indeed safe to assume that all who are affected by the conflict, regardless of their devotion to whatever faith they hold to, have questioned whether there is a worldview that gives meaning to such sorrow.

Second comes the demand for justice. Perhaps the most vehement outcry from Accad is about injustice. He is angry with Hezbollah, he is angry at Israel, he is angry with the international community, and he is angry with evangelicals for failing to look on the situation with an eye toward right and wrong. To be fair, however, Jews in Israel and here in America are quite baffled by the charges from some in the international community that its dealings in Lebanon and with the Palestinians are overly harsh. "Don't we have a right to defend our country?" they ask. "Don't we deserve justice in dealing with those who kill our children in the marketplace?" Similarly, Arabs and Muslims cry out for justice. "Is it just for the Israeli government to bulldoze our homes without being held accountable?" they ask. Time and again we hear both sides scream, "The sins wrought on us must be punished!" But the world, with all of its secular and relativistic trappings, has nothing to say to them about ultimate justice. Worse yet, it seems that the church, with its varying allegiances to end-times theologies, ignores the issue altogether.

Finally comes the desire for love. Feelings of sorrow and injustice naturally induce one to ask where love can be found. Arabs cry out, asking why Christians, who are supposed to follow a God who "is love," seem not to love them as they love Israel. I recall quite clearly my own desperate questions, wondering why Christians do not have unconditional love for my people or me. Perhaps the way in which I have recently heard the question put by other Muslims may put this into sharper focus: "Is there no love from Christians for us because we are not 'chosen'? Is there no room in their God's heart for us?"

The cries from Jews I have encountered are quite similar. Their entire history seems laced with suffering and persecution. As Accad acknowledges, Jews "have so suffered at the hands of others." After having been rounded up like sheep for slaughter in the recent past, Jews now have their own internationally recognized nation. Yet still they have no sense of security, and their children are still vulnerable to unspeakable violence. Just as Jews in the midst of the Holocaust questioned the existence of a God who could allow such a thing to happen, today's Jews ask how it can be that God loves them if He continues to allow them to suffer as they have.

The Opportunity of History

But in the midst of the anguish and pain felt by Arabs and Jews alike, there lies an opportunity for evangelicals to resolve the issues of sorrow, justice, and love in a profound spiritual sense. Indeed, it is poetically surprising that pain and suffering can actually bring about the greatest good. In his ingenious book, *The Problem of Pain*, C. S. Lewis artfully wrote,

> God whispers to us in our pleasures, speaks in our conscience, but shouts in our pain; it is His megaphone to rouse a deaf world.[3]

Here Lewis was addressing the argument used by skeptics to disprove God's existence. "If an all-powerful, all-loving God exists, He would use His limitless power and limitless love to do away with pain and evil," so the argument goes. Since evil and pain remain in the world, it must mean that there is no such all-powerful, all-loving being as God. Lewis points out the flaw in that argument. As limited, finite beings, humans cannot know whether there is some ultimate good that comes about from the existence of pain and suffering. Ultimately, what Lewis is saying goes beyond just a philosophical argument about God's existence. He is saying that our experiencing pain and evil can, in fact, be a good thing, because without it we would remain almost completely indifferent to our spiritual condition and our need for God. Indeed, it is our low spiritual condition that requires God to use the megaphone of pain to wake us up. God uses that megaphone to show us that He, rather than we, can provide resolution to our deepest struggles.

Recently, I read an article about a speech given by Tony Dungy, the head coach of the NFL champion Indianapolis Colts. Roughly a year before winning the NFL championship in 2007, Dungy gave a speech in Detroit and discussed the intense pain he and his family had endured and how that suffering had actually brought about real change in people's lives and glorified God. In that speech, Dungy spoke about his youngest son, who was born with a condition that prevents him from feeling pain:

> That sounds like it's good at the beginning, but I promise you it's not. We've learned a lot about pain in the last five years we've had Jordan. We've learned some hurts are really necessary for kids. Pain is necessary for kids to find out the difference between what's good and what's harmful.[4]

Dungy went on to profoundly answer why God allows pain in this life. "Sometimes," Dungy said, "pain is the only way that will turn us as kids back to the Father."[5]

Dungy then relayed the positive consequences resulting from the death of his oldest son, James. At the funeral, Dungy had given a beautiful eulogy. Afterward, a girl from his family's church sent him a letter that read, "When I saw what happened at the funeral and your family and the celebration and how it was handled, that was the first time I realized there had to be a God. I accepted Christ into my life and my life's been different since that day."[6]

Dungy realized that in the midst of his pain, God was shouting that sorrow and love and justice can find ultimate meaning in Him. Indeed, the parallel between Dungy's loss and the sacrifice of Jesus is not so hard to see. God gave up His only Son to die on the cross, realizing that a tremendous good, indeed the greatest good, would result.

The church is God's instrument on earth to spread his gospel. In other words, God has purposed us to *shout* on His behalf in the midst of the pain in the Holy Land to call all His children back to the Father. But the pain is not limited just to those actually living through the conflict. In the backyards of every American neighborhood and in the hallways of every American business and school, Arabs and Jews with ties to the Middle East are looking for answers to their own questions of sorrow, justice, and love. Sadly, they have not turned to the church for those answers. Why? Because the church is not *shouting* answers to their questions. Instead, evangelicals are shouting to Arabs and Jews that they are merely pawns in an end-times chess game.

As a Muslim, I heard those shouts loud and clear. But in the midst of those shouts, Christians who were concerned more with my salvation actually listened to my expressions of sorrow, my need for justice, and my desire for love. And when they shouted, they did not shout "Apocalypse Now!" They shouted the rationale and evidence for Jesus' crucifixion and resurrection and how those historic events ultimately resolved my struggles. Perhaps, then, the Church needs to change what it is shouting on God's behalf. Perhaps what God is "shouting to us in our pain" is not that we need to decide whether dispensationalists, Christian Zionists, or replacement theologians are interpreting prophecy correctly. Perhaps we need to focus on shouting the good news that Jesus, and He alone, resolves the issues of sorrow, justice, and love.

Interestingly, I have come to my local public library to get away from distractions so that I can finish this chapter. As I type, three college students are sitting at a table studying for an exam in their comparative religions course. I cannot help but overhear a girl in the group quizzing her friend on the fundamentals of Judaism, Christianity, Islam, Hinduism, and Buddhism. I have studied those same fundamentals of those same religions. Indeed, I have now lived and breathed the fundamentals of two of those worldviews. As those college students drone over the facts about these worldviews, I wonder if the members of that trio have considered whether any of the worldviews they are so dryly studying offers any cohesive answer to the conflict and strife we see and experience all around us every day. Just as I complete the previous sentence, the girl quizzes her friend, "What is the basic set of moral laws in the Judeo-Christian view?"

Her friend pipes up, "The Ten Commandments."

"That's right," she replies. "I wonder if we have to know all ten for the test," she says anxiously.

One of Jesus' disciples, Matthew, wrote in his Gospel of an incident when Jesus was similarly quizzed over two thousand years ago.

> Then one of them, a lawyer, asked *Him a question*, testing Him, and saying, "Teacher, which *is* the great commandment in the law?" (Matt. 22:35–36)

Jesus did not rebuke the man for being knowledgeable about the 613 laws in the Torah that governed Jewish life. Nor did He applaud him for knowing them so well. But as only Jesus can so masterfully do, He showed this lawyer that for all his preoccupation with the corpus and details of the law, he missed that which is so fundamental to all of those laws.

> Jesus said to him, "'You shall love the Lord your God with all your heart, with all your soul, and with all your mind.' This is *the* first and great commandment. And *the* second is like it: 'You shall love your neighbor as yourself.' On these two commandments hang all the Law and the Prophets." (Matt. 22:37–40)

Knowing the breadth of biblical issues is a good and grand thing. But as Jesus pointed out to the lawyer, if the preoccupation with the breadth replaces our zeal for the depth, then our preoccupation is unhealthy and we will miss something even grander.

To be sure, eschatological issues are important. Indeed, when interpreted correctly and discussed in a balanced way, they can be quite illuminating. But as Christians, we have become bogged down in the preoccupation with whether a certain current event will be ushering in the Apocalypse. By doing so, we risk losing sight of that most fundamental of commandments that Jesus gave His church after His resurrection: "Go therefore and make disciples of all the nations, baptizing them in the name of the Father and of the Son and of the Holy Spirit" (Matt. 28:19–20). The beauty of Jesus' command is that it encompasses the commandment to love God and to love our neighbors as ourselves. Fulfillment of the Great Commission at once honors God and shows our neighbors that we love them so deeply that we take the time and effort to offer them Christ.

If the real "test" in this life is about how Christians respond to the cries of sorrow, the demand for justice, and the pleas for love that emanate from the Middle East Conflict, then I pray that our conversation with the nonbelieving world does not build more walls. I pray that our conversation is about the first, best thing the church can do—preach Christ and Him crucified. The church's ardent involvement in spreading the gospel is a missing piece of the Middle East puzzle. As I hope to show in the coming chapters, it is Jesus of Nazareth, the subject of that gospel, who is the missing piece of the missing peace in the Middle East.

Chapter 2

STUMBLING BLOCKS

Jesus or Eschatology?

Distrusting in Two-Part Harmony

Several years ago, I gave a presentation at a church in the Detroit, Michigan, area titled, "What Is Truth?" The purpose of my presentation was to explore the topic of truth, whether it can be known, and whether the Christian faith has any basis in it. The event was geared, not just to Christians, but also to non-Christians looking for answers. The facility was packed to capacity. As the event proceeded, I scanned the audience, wondering who in the crowd had come with sincere doubts and questions that they wanted—perhaps desperately needed—answers to.

Inevitably, after every speaking engagement, people from the audience will approach me, seeking more explanation on a topic that I covered. Sometimes, however, a person has no intention of discussing the night's topic. Instead, the questioner wants to raise a different issue, often one that has been burning in the person's heart and mind for some time. After the presentation that evening, the audience was invited to meet in a gathering hall for food and refreshments. As I walked to that hall, I wondered who would approach me and what their questions might be. I had just begun to drink my soda when a young man approached me, asking if I would talk to his friend.

"He's a Muslim, and he's asking a lot of really great questions," he told me. "Will you talk with him alone?" Although I very much enjoy talking with Christians after a speaking engagement, I relish the chance to engage non-Christians in the discussion of important ideas. I agreed and went to meet the young man's friend.

As we exchanged pleasantries, I learned that the young Muslim man was Palestinian. Our conversation began with a discussion of the evidence for Christianity that I had presented that evening. It soon became apparent, however, that although this man was sincerely searching, he remained confrontational. He left no point I made unchallenged, even if it meant that his challenge would not be a very good one or was poorly thought out. This is not uncommon in my experience dealing with non-Christians, even the most intelligent of them. I sometimes deal with thoughtful objections, but I am also confronted with arguments that are so poor that just stating the argument back to the person is enough to point out its flaws. Interestingly, there are times when thoughtful and poor challenges come from the same person. I have discovered that otherwise intelligent people often bring weak challenges, not for any lack of ability but because of emotional baggage. For each of us, as our objections are answered one by one, our fear of losing the argument, or of losing our basis for holding onto our previous position, leads us to throw any challenge we can muster at the wall in hopes that something might stick. I am all too familiar with this phenomenon. Some of my own objections to Christianity when I was still a Muslim stemmed from my fears that Christianity just might be true. For many a Muslim, the fear of the consequences in the family if a decision is made to follow Jesus is simply too much to consider. But this is not a phenomenon particular to Muslims, of course. Jews, Hindus, Buddhists, and yes, even so-called nonreligious agnostics or atheists face similar costs when sincerely considering Christ's claims.

Cognizant of this, I assumed that this Muslim man's emotional baggage centered on his family. He quickly disproved

my assumption when he told me that he had been estranged
from his family for years and that it would make no difference to them whether he remained a Muslim from a spiritual
standpoint. Still, I wondered what had caused him to be so
confrontational in our discussion. What drove this otherwise
intelligent, erudite young man to bring up even silly challenges, no matter how they might sound? I decided to wait for
him to reveal it to me. And then it came.

"Do you, as a Christian, think that everything Israel does is
right?" he asked me intensely. "If so, don't you feel like you're
betraying your own people?"

I was expecting this issue to come up eventually. The Middle
East conflict will *always* come up with a Muslim in these contexts. But still, I was momentarily taken aback by the intensity of his tone and the piercing look in his eyes as he asked.
He continued, "You're an Arab; in fact you're Lebanese. But my
friend who brought me here tells me that as a Christian, you
have to support the State of Israel no matter what it does to
the Palestinians or the Lebanese. He tells me that you have to
believe this because biblical prophecy is being fulfilled by the
events in Palestine, and supporting Israel supports Jesus' return. Now, you talked tonight about how God's justice required
Jesus to pay the penalty for sin, but from what I see, there isn't
any justice in Christianity."

The man's pointed question was based on only a caricature
of what dispensational eschatology teaches about Israel and
the last days. Indeed, it was based on a caricature of a subset
of dispensationalism, called Christian Zionism. But that caricature had been repeatedly shouted to him from every angle.
Because he perceived the heart of Christianity this way, his
was a passion-filled question and an important question. The
passion stemmed from the agony of his wounds. The importance stemmed from the fact that his perceptions are so commonly held by others.

In my experience, I had fielded many off-topic questions that
were designed to divert attention away from the main topic.

But this time, the pathos behind the question was fundamentally and profoundly different. How should I answer? How could I get us back to the original, fundamental topic of the person of Christ and His resurrection without appearing to sidestep this man's question?

Not long after that encounter, I was speaking with a Jewish friend over lunch about the controversy surrounding the soon-to-be-released movie, *The Passion of the Christ*. In the weeks before the film's release, the media had made much hay of the allegations by some that it was anti-Semitic. I asked him if he intended to see the film. He answered that he felt obligated to. "If I'm going to decide for myself whether it has an anti-Semitic bent," he said, "I should actually see it. But I'm nervous about going."

I asked him why he was nervous, and he told me, "I'm just not sure what the attitude of mainstream Christians is toward Jews." He went on to tell me how he felt the history of Christendom's dealings with Jews had taught him to be apprehensive.

Curious, I asked him, "Does the prevailing attitude in the Western church in supporting Israel as strongly as it does cause you to trust Christians more?"

"Not really," he said. "I'm not convinced that Christians 'love' Israel for the sake of Jews. I think that to a lot of Christians, Jews are important to them only because they somehow figure in to the Christians' view about the end of the world and Jesus' coming back." That statement from my Jewish friend was just as impassioned and filled with pathos as the question the Palestinian man had asked me a few months before.

The question from the Palestinian and the statement from my Jewish friend could not have come from two more different people and perspectives. Yet, the challenge they presented to me was the same. The challenge was not just to answer a question or respond to a statement. My fundamental challenge, my first challenge, was to determine what had brought these men to the places where I had found them.

I would only have to delve into my recent past as a Muslim to identify with these men. In the years before I made my decision to follow Jesus, I had become distrustful of Christians' motivations whenever they spoke to me. I had the distinct feeling that they distrusted me because of my own background, especially because I was a Muslim. In some sense, their distrust arose from the apprehensions I generated. Perhaps I had a political chip on my own shoulder. As I talked with Christians, I would wait for the Middle East Conflict to come up. In doing so, I would often ignore the spiritual message they gave me, if any. Usually, however, I would not have to wait very long before I would hear something that would confirm my suspicions that Christians viewed my people as an obstacle to the fulfillment of prophecy. With this bit of introspection, I understood that to reach the Palestinian man and to reach my Jewish friend, I had to see what they were hearing when the church spoke to them.

Seeing What They Hear

The Palestinian had been living and going to school in the United States for several years. He had befriended a devout Christian, who had brought him to my presentation that evening. But despite living in a peaceful environment in the United States and despite his close relationship with someone of a different faith, he had no peace. That very evening, he had heard the unadulterated gospel and evidence that sustained it, but he had not actually listened to it. Why?

My Jewish friend, with whom I've shared the gospel many times, still had no peace within himself. He had conceded on several occasions that the evidence for the gospel was compelling. But in his last statement to me over lunch, I had learned that he had not actually been taking it in. Why?

As a Lebanese former Muslim, it was not hard for me to see what the Palestinian man had heard from the church. Nor was it difficult to understand how my Jewish friend, as a non-Christian, could bypass looking at the gospel and instead see a political agenda within Christianity. My own experience and encounters with non-Christians have convinced me that many times when the gospel is given to non-Christians, especially Muslims or Jews, they are not really hearing the message. I am not suggesting that they are being rude or ignoring Christians. Quite the opposite—I have often found them to be polite and engaging. What I am suggesting is that they have a misperception about the church's motives and the consequences of its message. When the Christian says that "God so loved the world that He gave His only begotten Son" to die in payment of our sins, they perceive something quite different. The message is drowned out by the booming voices or long missives from Christians on the radio, television, or in print saying that Jews or Arabs are either excluded from the culmination of God's plan for the last days or are valuable only because they figure into making those last days come about.

As I spoke to the young Palestinian man, I concluded that the in-house Christian debate over the end times and how the Israeli-Arab conflict figured in was still echoing in his head. Have we seen what they hear us saying? Noted Christian Zionist and political author Michael Evans has written that Palestinians are "a tainted and brainwashed people."[1] I recall quite vividly hearing a well-known Christian speaker during a radio broadcast say that if Muslims opposed the reconstruction of Solomon's temple in Jerusalem, violently or otherwise, the West ought to use its nuclear capabilities to make Mecca a "black spot" on the map. The Western church certainly had engaged the Palestinian man and his culture, but it had not shouted the gospel of grace and salvation in spite of sin. It had shouted something sensationalistic and off-putting. It had shouted about how every event or political move in the Middle East was foretold in the Scriptures.

My Jewish friend had perceived much the same thing. He disclosed to me that he had heard from one camp in the church that Jews no longer had significance in God's redemptive plan.

From another camp, he had heard how special Jews were, but he had heard this primarily in the context of the details of the end times. And, yes, he had heard that in the "Time of Jacob's Trouble," the tribulation that will precede Jesus' physical return, two-thirds of all Jews will be killed, because of their "national blood-guiltiness" for the "murder of Christ."[2] In fact, David Brickner, the executive director for Jews for Jesus, recently wrote, "One might think that Jewish people, especially Jewish leaders, would welcome Christian support for the State of Israel—and many do." Brickner goes on to note, however, that there is a "large swath of the Jewish community that suspects the motives of Christian Zionism."[3] Brickner quoted a leading progressive Jewish leader, Rabbi Michael Lerner, who commented that Jews are suspicious of Christians' interest in Jews and Israel because Jews perceive Christians as believing only "that getting Israel into a huge battle with the Arab states is going to be good for bringing Jesus back onto our planet."[4] Thus, from one camp, Jews like my friend hear that they are seemingly insignificant to the future. From another camp, they hear that Jews have a profound but gruesome significance in future events.

What is the Jew to think hearing such words? What is the Arab to make of what Christians think about him and his family when such statements are made? Although there may be some merit in some details of the argument being advanced by the proponents of the various eschatological views, the old adage holds true that it is not so much *what* is said but *how* it is said that really makes the impact. In our day, distrust of active Christianity is not a matter of the details that are being debated within Christian orthodoxy but how the debate is articulated in the public square. I fear that Muslims, Jews, and other non-Christians refuse to consider the details of biblical prophecy regarding Messiah's return, not because the topic itself is off-putting, but because it has been given a stinging, ethnically charged tone.

The charge has been that evangelicals are more focused

on religio-political issues than on truly ministering to the
souls affected by the longest-running and most fearsome conflict in recorded history. Non-Christians, especially Jews and
Muslims, are keenly sensitive to Christian attitudes toward
the conflict and how they affect the issues of sorrow, justice,
and love. Non-Christians are so sensitive to what the church
says in this context that they tend to overemphasize the political and eschatological messages over the fundamental
message of the gospel. But in so doing, they are only mirror-
ing evangelicals' emphases. While we speak of salvation and
reconciliation through Christ, we shout about politics and eschatological agendas. But the Bible challenges us to shift our
focus. In Acts 1, the disciples asked Jesus after His resurrection whether He would now restore the kingdom to Israel (Acts
1:6). Jesus admonished them to focus on preaching the gospel
to a lost world. "It is not for you to know times or epochs which
the Father has fixed by His own authority," Jesus said. "But
you will receive power when the Holy Spirit has come upon
you; and you shall be My witnesses both in Jerusalem, and in
all Judea and Samaria, and even to the remotest part of the
earth" (Acts 1:7–8 NASB).

We must see what others hear us saying. Only when that is
done can we shift the focus of what we are saying. And when
we shift the focus of what we are saying, we must undertake
the challenge of getting others to see what we are saying. John
R. W. Stott put it well when he wrote, "One of the greatest arts
or gifts in gospel-preaching is to turn people's ears into eyes,
and to make them *see* what we are talking about."[5]

Will the Real Stumbling Block Please Stand Up?

The gospel itself is a stumbling block (see 1 Cor. 1:22–25).
With an unabashed honesty, the Bible declares this fact about
its central message. It does not hide from the reality that its
truths are profound, yet difficult for us to embrace. Where
other worldviews might downplay the difficulties within their

respective systems, the Bible is refreshingly, even uniquely, forthright about that which is most difficult about the gospel to embrace.

As a matter of logic, the existence of difficulty in a worldview's central message is not a sufficient reason to reject it. In fact, I daresay that sometimes difficulty actually may be a sign that the worldview is worth sincere examination. Is it not common experience that the path of least resistance is often the path of least substance? As the saying goes, nothing worthwhile is easy. Whether in matters of intellectual, artistic, athletic, or spiritual pursuits, it is usually the case that hardship and difficulty lead to true positive results. With respect to difficulty in the gospel, the famed English writer G. K. Chesterton once wrote, "The Christian ideal has not been tried and found wanting; it has been found difficult and left untried."[6]

Of course, it is one thing for a worldview to be difficult to embrace because its truths are profound and beautifully complex. It is quite another thing for a worldview to be difficult to grasp because its basic tenets are incoherent. In our intellectual laziness concerning spirituality, we have resorted to labeling confusing or self-contradictory worldviews as "deep" or "mysterious." The marketplace of ideas offers us many worldviews with pretentious ideas and supposed depth that are really just contradictory and vacuous sentiments wrapped in sophisticated packaging.

But the "difficulty" in the gospel message does not stem from seemingly contradictory claims or incoherent dogma. Nor is the difficulty found in the complexity of Christian doctrine. It is true that there are difficult doctrines in Christianity, such as the Trinity, the incarnation, and perhaps even Christ's substitutionary atonement. But the primary difficulty in accepting the gospel arises from its indictments of the human heart and its proclamation that humanity is incapable of saving itself. If the gospel is true, then every man, woman, and child is spiritually dead, and nothing they can do can improve their situation. It takes the saving work of Christ to make us alive to God. To the human heart, that means that we cannot rely on ourselves to engineer a better future. And we have tremendous difficulty letting go of our own sense of merit.

Unflinchingly, the gospel proclaims itself to be a stumbling stone to humanity:

> For indeed Jews ask for signs and Greeks[7] search for wisdom; but we preach Christ crucified, to Jews a stumbling block and to Gentiles foolishness, but to those who are the called, both Jews and Greeks, Christ the power of God and the wisdom of God. Because the foolishness of God is wiser than men, and the weakness of God is stronger than men. (1 Cor. 1:22–25 NASB)

The apostle Paul, history's greatest and most ardent Christian missionary, was inspired to pen those words. The context of this passage is Paul's address to the Corinthian church, which he himself founded in one of the most licentious Greek cities in the Roman Empire. In the time since Paul had left them to continue on his mission, the Corinthians had fallen back into egregious spiritual error, not the least of which was their bickering about whom among the early leaders they should follow. Some boasted that they followed Apollos, others Cephas, and still others, Paul (1 Cor. 1:10–13). They were focusing heavily on who among the leaders of the church had baptized them. But ever mindful of the centrality of the gospel of Jesus Christ, Paul sought to put an end to their bickering by pointing out that it was not important who had baptized them and it was equally unimportant which man they had given their allegiance to. The important thing, Paul said, was the fundamental gospel.

Paul's reference to the stumbling block comes in this context and informs us that the gospel itself is enough of a stumbling block without the church having to put more blocks in the way.[8] In fact, in the same letter to the Corinthians, Paul calls them to focus on the simplicity and centrality of the fundamental gospel.

> For I delivered to you first of all that which I also received: that Christ died for our sins according to the Scriptures, and that He was buried, and that He rose again the third day according to the Scriptures, and that He was seen by Cephas, then by the twelve. After that He was seen by over five hundred brethren at once, of whom the greater part remain to the present, but some have fallen asleep. After that He was seen by James, then by all the apostles. Then last of all He was seen by me also, as by one born out of due time. (1 Cor. 15:3–8)

This passage is a proclamation of the bare gospel, unadorned by flowery language, made plain to the Corinthians, who were so poisoned by peripheral (even sinful) issues that they needed undiluted medicine. If a body of believers instituted by the greatest missionary in history could stumble over extraneous matters, how easy is it for today's church to stumble over nonessentials and to cause nonbelievers to do the same? How much easier is it, then, for non-Christians to stumble over our in-house debates and never get to the gospel itself?

As an expression of the essential Gospel, 1 Corinthians 15:3–8 is important for additional reasons. First, it is one of the earliest communiqués of the gospel to the burgeoning church. Scholars, both Christian and non-Christian, place the date of Paul's visit to the Corinthians (when he "delivered" this gospel to them) at around A.D. 51, less than twenty years after Jesus' crucifixion.[9] Thus, Paul discusses the basics of the gospel, not just as a theological matter, but also as a *historical one*, well within the very generation that would have witnessed the events Paul was describing. In fact, Paul's reference to the witness of "five hundred brethren," most of whom were still alive, was his way of challenging the reader to verify Paul's assertions by going to the living eyewitnesses themselves.

Second, scholars have almost uniformly affirmed that in this passage Paul is quoting early creedal information that predates 1 Corinthians by decades. This information is contained in the passage beginning, "For I delivered to you first of all that which I also received." In fact, many scholars believe that Paul "received" this creedal information from Peter and James between A.D. 31 and 33. This fact, coupled with the very un-Pauline structure of the passage, has led scholars of every stripe to conclude that the passage originated from the earliest Christian creeds, possibly originating within just eighteen months of the crucifixion.[10]

This leads to the conclusion that this earliest formulation of the gospel is primary both in time and in substance. In fact, in verse 3, Paul writes that he is delivering this information "first of all." This phrase comes from the Greek word *protos*, which means first in time and first in rank, influence, or importance. The phrase has been translated "of first importance" (NIV). For the burgeoning first-century church, there was nothing more primitive than this creed, nor was anything more primary than its substance.

The passage's straightforward creedal format, coupled with its extremely early origins, highlights its expression as the fundamental gospel, stripped down to its bare essentials. Before any doctrinal disputes arose, before eschatological disputes dominated the scene, the message found in 1 Corinthians 15—the stumbling block that trips up all nonbelievers—was the message the first Christians, indeed the very disciples of Jesus, shouted to the non-Christian world.

In his first letter, the apostle Peter, a disciple handpicked by Jesus, calls Jesus Himself a stumbling block. In speaking of Jesus, Peter extensively quotes from the Old Testament.

> Therefore it is also contained in the Scripture, "Behold, I lay in Zion a chief cornerstone, elect, precious, and he who believes on Him will by no means be put to shame."
> Therefore, to you who believe, He is precious; but to

those who are disobedient, "The stone which the builders rejected has become the chief cornerstone," and "A stone of stumbling and a rock of offense." (1 Peter 2:6–8)

It is interesting that Peter was inspired to use the "stone" and "stumbling block" metaphors, when years before, Jesus had called him the "rock" (Matt. 16:18). But the Scripture tells us that Peter the Rock tripped over the stumbling block of Jesus' fundamental purpose for coming to earth. The Gospel writers tell us that after Peter had answered Jesus' question about His identity correctly, Jesus began to tell the disciples that He would be crucified. Peter, ever loyal yet rash, actually rebuked Jesus for thinking such a thought. Peter was a fighter and had his own ideas about what it meant for Jesus to be the Christ. It seems likely that in those first few years, Peter saw Jesus as one who would overcome Israel's Roman conquerors and "restore the kingdom to Israel" within just a short while. The idea that Jesus would die an excruciating and humiliating death at the hands of the very ones Peter sought to vanquish was simply abhorrent. Like many of us today, Peter's political or ideological agenda overshadowed his ability to really grasp the depth of Jesus' true mission. Jesus responded sternly to Peter's objection, saying, "Get behind Me, Satan! You are a stumbling block to Me" (Matt. 16:23 NASB). Leading New Testament scholars commenting on Jesus and Peter's exchange put it well.

It is noteworthy that Matthew adds this reference to Peter's being a stumbling block, since it is he alone who, in the preceding paragraph, reports Jesus' words about the rock. There are two kinds of rock here: there is a kind of rock which provides a stable foundation, and there is the kind of rock which lies in the way and trips people up. Indeed, one and the same rock can sometimes fulfill both functions.

Peter had it in him to be either a foundation stone or

a stumbling block. Thanks to the intercession which his
Master made for him in a critical hour, he strengthened
his brethren (Luke 22:32) and became a rock of stability
and a focus of unity.[11]

I would add another noteworthy aspect here. After Jesus'
rebuke, and after having witnessed Jesus' resurrection, Peter
came to understand the fundamental gospel. He understood
that it was Jesus who humiliated death, not the other way
around. With this revealed truth and his own experience in
mind, Peter tells us that Jesus himself, and the truth of His
redemptive work on the cross, are stumbling blocks for those
who have ideas or agendas that differ with this most basic
facet of the gospel.

It was during those first glorious yet tempestuous years
that the gospel made its greatest gains. Even at times when
the numbers of conversions were not impressive, the sheer
fact that any conversions happened at all caused the church
to marvel. Born in a hostile religious culture and under the
banner of a hostile Roman political machine, Christianity
steadily advanced in the hearts and minds of both populaces.
Is it not remarkable that the gospel would succeed despite its
self-admitted status as a great stumbling block? This success
happened because the first believers shared the truth of the
basic gospel. It was the message they lived and died for.

That kind of powerful success escapes us today because we
do not shout the gospel and the reasons for its truth to the nonbelieving world. Instead, we shout many, many other things.
We shout about "prosperity," we shout about "a better life." But
to those most resistant to Christianity, Jews and Muslims, we
shout about prophecy, ethnicity, and land entitlement. Jews
and Muslims do not hear that they are invited to have a place
in God's kingdom in the sense that they, too, can be redeemed
and have salvation. Instead, they are invited to take their
place as game pieces in the end-times chess match unfolding
before our eyes.

In the eschatological dialogue, we are not just shouting academic doctrinal points. No, we are shouting specific messages that have lasting impact on the hearers. In discussing the eschatological consequences of the Jewish rejection of Jesus as Messiah, one scholar has said that one such consequence will be "the death of two-thirds of the flock. This will be fulfilled during the Great Tribulation when Israel will suffer tremendous persecution (Matt. 24:15–28; Rev. 12:1–17). As a result of this persecution of the Jewish people, two-thirds are going to be killed."[12] What is the non-messianic Jew who is being asked to consider the claims of Christ to make of this statement? Is there a message of hope and reconciliation on the face of such a message? Should this be *shouted* while the exclusive saving power of the gospel is only *spoken?*

Just a few years ago, I was at a Muslim family's home in the United States, visiting just after the funeral of a dear loved one. As is usually the case when more than one Arab is in the room, the Middle East Conflict became the main topic of discussion. Shortly into the conversation, they began to express their anger at certain Christian leaders who were encouraging political and military advances against Arab interests. Their anger was focused on their perception that these Christians were interested only in hastening Jesus' second coming and cared nothing for the Arabs' plight. Naturally, they aimed their ire at a caricature of dispensationalism. They made fun of it, perhaps as a defense mechanism that derides an idea instead of engaging its merits. Struggle as I did, I could not turn them away from their opinions. Though I tried to show not only that they had a skewed view of dispensationalism but also that there was another eschatological view in Christianity, my efforts were summarily dismissed. It quickly became apparent that the loudest voice in that home that day was not going to center on the gospel but on end-times sensationalism. Those men had stumbled, but not over the gospel. Indeed, they had stumbled long before our discussion that day.

The end result is that non-Christians, Jews and Muslims,

stumble over the eschatologically fueled geopolitical theory that influences so much of what goes on in that part of the world. And as my conversations with the young Palestinian man, my Jewish friend, and the mourning Muslims showed, those living in our backyards are profoundly affected. This very day, 35,000 Muslims will die without hearing the gospel.[13] A proportionate number of Jews will die today without hearing that same gospel, and the number of other nonbelievers who will die today without Jesus as their Savior must be nothing short of staggering. If even one soul is worth our focusing on the gospel rather than the nonessentials that divide us, how much more should the millions who die lost give us pause to consider the Great Commission above all else?

History's Debates Repeat Themselves

It is natural and quite right that Christians should engage in the debate over what the Bible says about the last days and Jesus' second coming. After all, the Bible has a great deal to say about these issues. And regardless of one's worldview or faith, the Bible is an ancient, hugely important document that has shaped the course of history and promises to shape the future. As such, no part of it is superfluous or unworthy of our attention.

And so throughout the ages many have studied what the Bible has to say about Jesus' second coming and the end of days that leads up to it. The early church viewed Jesus' second coming as connected to His first. Jesus taught that His first coming was the event that inaugurated the beginning of the end. In fact, we read that He was the "firstborn" of the resurrection of the dead (Col. 1:18). Historically, most Jews believed that at the end of time, God will raise the dead to life. Having witnessed Jesus' resurrection, the early Jewish Christians understood that God had begun the process by which the entire world, including the Gentile world, will be part of the general resurrection on the Last Day.

The debate over what Jesus and the apostles meant with respect to the details of the events leading up to the Second Coming has raged on within evangelical Christianity, and various schools of thought have emerged. For simplicity's sake, I will not detail the various issues and explanations within each school and sub-school. Suffice it to say that one of the main schools of thought on the end times asserts that Jesus and the apostles had referred to a great tribulation that would directly affect their contemporary generation, resulting in the destruction of Jerusalem and the temple in A.D. 70 by the Romans. Another school of thought says that Jesus and the apostles meant that the tribulation would occur in a much more distant future in the last days. Despite the debate, it is clear (and agreed upon by all camps) that Jesus had come once, and that His resurrection ushered in a time when He would come again. All agree that His second coming will be the culminating event of the end times.

Heavy-hitting, well-respected scholars are found in all the camps. They have compellingly argued their respective cases and have convinced thousands to join their respective positions. But how can it be that so many well-respected scholars within Christian orthodoxy can disagree (and so sharply) over this issue?[14] There are major differences among the views, but there are also many similarities. The similarities are essential to the Christian faith, so that in the end one looking objectively at Christianity could not conclude that it is flawed even though the faith's scholars debate nonessential and perhaps unclear details regarding eschatological issues. The fact is, these scholars do agree on a most essential fact—that Jesus will physically return in the future. It is in the details of His return and the place the nation Israel has in that return that the disagreement lies. But somehow, despite the broad agreement, it is the debate over the eschatological details that have become one of the most visible faces of Christianity to the non-Christian world.

The non-Christian world's penchant for focusing on the

negatives is one reason why the debate has become so visible. But the church has fueled this perception as well. Premillennialists, which includes dispensationalists, believe Christ will return to establish a thousand-year kingdom on earth. They have interpreted 1 Thessalonians 4 to depict a sudden rapture of the church out of the world. Yet, even within the ranks of premillenialism, scholars differ on whether that Rapture will occur before, during, or after the "great tribulation" that the world will undergo in the last days. Differing over this, premillennialists have hurled vitriol on one another. In his essay "A History of the Development of the Rapture Positions," Richard Reiter cites a statement by a leading scholar who holds to the post-tribulation rapture as saying of pretribulationists: "Wherever I am I smite that God dishonoring Doctrine."[15] This is but one example of how we have made the debate over the details about Jesus' second coming, and which ethnic groups will figure into those details, our most apparent message to the non-Christian world.

We in the Western church are debating these details among ourselves so vehemently that outsiders hear nothing else. I liken the current furor of this debate to a home where the family sharply argues from time to time. As neighbors walk by that home, they hear the family members inside loudly arguing with each other. An occasional argument might be seen as a typical "in-house" argument. But the more frequent the arguments and the more vociferous the exchanges, the more the outsiders come to feel that disagreement and strife, not harmony, dominate the family relationships. The neighbors and other outsiders might get this impression even if the number of arguments pales in comparison to the number of good times. Yet the intensity of the family feuds communicates far more than the tranquility of the unity. Here is the point: While debate over nonessentials is important and even healthy, unrestrained and unbalanced argument drowns out the core messages we so desperately want to share.

But is the visibility and volatility—or rather the visibility *of*

the volatility—warranted? Jesus' first advent, His death, and
His resurrection are part of the gospel and hailed the beginning of the end times in a general sense. For centuries before
Jesus' birth, the rabbis and learned among the Jews studied
the prophecies concerning the Messiah's coming. Looking to
the Torah, the writings of David, and the prophets like Ezekiel,
Daniel, Isaiah, and others, intelligent and influential leaders
within the community became divided into two camps about
the nature of the Messiah and his advent. A minority group
saw that the Scriptures prophesied and described the Messiah
as a suffering servant.[16] Looking to passages such as Psalm
22, Isaiah 53, Daniel 9:26, and others, this group saw the
Messiah as one who, like Jacob's son, Joseph, would patiently
endure suffering for the sake of the people. Seeing this, rabbis
eventually came to title him *Messiah Ben Joseph*.[17] Indeed, the
tradition about Messiah Ben Joseph saw him not just as one
who suffers for the people, but as one who also dies for them.[18]

But another equally learned and influential group among
the Hebrews also combed the Scriptures for glimpses of the
Anointed One. Finding Psalms 2, 45, and 110, Micah 5, Isaiah
9, Jeremiah 23:5–8, Daniel 7:13–18, and other passages to be
filled with triumphant tones and royal archetypes, this group
saw the Messiah as a conquering king who would usher in an
era of prosperity and godliness. To them, the Messiah was not
a lowly servant who would suffer for God's people. No, he would
conquer in God's name for their sake. Seeing this, they named
the coming Anointed One in accordance with his descendancy
from Israel's greatest ruler, giving him the moniker *Messiah
Ben David*.[19]

Thus, in the first century, some waited for the coming of the
suffering Messiah Ben Joseph. Still others longed to see the
coming of the conquering Messiah Ben David, who would free
them from the oppression of the Roman Empire. Indeed, even
Jesus' closest followers adamantly clung to the view that he had
come to "redeem" Israel from its oppression under Roman rule
(Luke 24:21) and "restore the kingdom to Israel" (Acts 1:6).

But as we look back on the person and work of Jesus Christ, we see that neither of these two views was completely correct. Both views contained profound truths about the Messiah. But both had a serious shortcoming in failing to see that they both had the essentials correct. Both were right, and both were wrong. The Messiah was both suffering servant and conquering king. On the Emmaus road, Jesus encountered His disciples, who were downtrodden about Jesus' crucifixion. They did not realize that Jesus was talking to them, when they said in their grief over His death, "But we were hoping that it was He who was going to redeem Israel" (Luke 24:21 NASB). Jesus confronted the disciples' incredulity over His death. He assured them that the Messiah had to die, but He also assured them that the Messiah's purpose was to ultimately reign as King. "Was it not necessary for the Christ to suffer these things *and* to enter into His glory?" Jesus said to them (Luke 24:26 NASB, emphasis added). The Jews had debated the question, "Would Messiah be a suffering servant or a Davidic king?" Jesus' answer was, "Yes."

Is it not possible that the same situation exists today with respect to the end-times debate? There are Bible-believing, astute scholars on all sides of the argument, and they truly believe in the glory of God the Father through his Son. It may be that all of their views have elements that should be explored, debated, and discussed. And it may be they are all partly right and all partly wrong. If that be the case, then the risk we take in making this debate so prevalent that it overshadows the gospel is unwarranted. Perhaps de-emphasizing the eschatological debate is in order.

Indeed, the apostle John illustrates for us how clinging to one view of the Messiah's nature can lead to disillusionment. In chapter 12 of his Gospel, John recounts Jesus' triumphal entry into Jerusalem. The timing was powerfully enticing to the hopes of the oppressed Jewish populace. Just before their greatest holiday commemorating their deliverance by God from Egyptian bondage, Jesus had proved His power over death by raising Lazarus from the dead. Now, Jesus rode into Jerusalem, the City of David, in the manner of the king, as described by the prophet Zechariah (Zech. 9:9). Emotionally intoxicated by the possibility that Jesus would soon do away with the Roman rulers, the Jewish populace welcomed Him as their King.

> The next day a great multitude that had come to the feast, when they heard that Jesus was coming to Jerusalem, took branches of palm trees and went out to meet Him, and cried out:
>   *"Hosanna!*
>   *'Blessed is He who comes in the name of the Lord!'*
>   *The King of Israel!"*
>
> Then Jesus, when He had found a young donkey, sat on it; as it is written:
>   *"Fear not, daughter of Zion;*
>   *Behold, your King is coming,*
>   *Sitting on a donkey's colt."*
>
> His disciples did not understand these things at first; but when Jesus was glorified, then they remembered that these things were written about Him and *that* they had done these things to Him. (John 12:12–16)

Just days later, many in that same crowd would see their conquering King suffer the ignominy of death on a Roman cross. Feeling that Jesus would not fulfill their expectations of conquest, the crowd demanded that the Romans execute Him and that Barabbas, an incarcerated murderer, be released from Roman custody in His place. The fact that the crowd would rather have a murderous man released into their midst illustrates the anger they felt toward Jesus because of their disappointment over what appeared to be yet another failed, would-be deliverer (Matt. 27:15–26; Mark 15:6–15).

The crowd had missed Jesus' dual role as both Messiah Ben Joseph and Messiah Ben David because they had focused so heavily on only one view of Him. Is it not strange that the eyewitnesses to Jesus' first coming could not see the unfolding good news because of their zealous adherence to one view of the Messiah's first coming, yet we, looking through the annals of history, see it so clearly? Is it not ironic that we, who see His first coming so clearly, now block others from seeing it because of our own staunch adherence to one view of His second coming?

Shouting in Two-Part Harmony

The preaching of the gospel is the most important aspect of the Christian exchange with the non-Christian world. Is not the salvation of souls so important that we should lower the volume of our in-house debates so that outsiders can hear the pure gospel? As C. S. Lewis so clearly stated, "The salvation of a single soul is more important than the production or preservation of all the epics and tragedies in the world."[20]

Despite the many, many books that have been written about the Last Day, some of the details are still shrouded in mystery. In the midst of our uncertainty, the "end result," the salvation of all who believe regardless of ethnicity, is the most important and central aspect of Christianity. Christianity is not exclusivist in terms of those who are invited to be saved (although it is exclusive in terms of how). The salvation of the entire world is ultimately important. The importance of the speculative details we posit as to exactly how and when Jesus' second coming will occur pale in comparison.

What is most telling is that the eschatological debate, and the debate over which ethnicity is entitled to "the Land," causes rifts not just between Christians and non-Christians, but especially among Christians. Quite a bit has been written on the subject of the sharply differing views held by Jewish Christians and Arab Christians. In her short but informative article, "Differing Eschatological Viewpoints: Obstacles to Relationship?" Lisa Loden, a messianic Jew, summarizes the various and intensely contrary eschatological views held among Christians. She explains how these differences have kept Jewish believers and Arab believers from coming together in fellowship and understanding. But Jewish and Arab believers are coming to terms with their eschatological differences and seeing their commonality as believers redeemed under the blood of Christ. Loden quotes Baruch Moaz, another notable messianic Jew, on this point.

> Christians may differ in matters of where and when or in what sequence this or that aspect of eschatology will be fulfilled. Nevertheless, they are our brethren in Christ and should be acknowledged as such. Differences of opinion in these areas ought never to be allowed to infringe upon the integrity or fullness of our fellowship. Hence, however great an importance we attach to those issues, we tacitly recognize that they do not form the essential substance of our faith.[21]

Indeed, this is telling. If the eschatological controversy is a barrier to reconciliation among Christians, how much more insurmountable is this barrier to the gospel in the sight of non-Christians? Perhaps, then, Moaz's admonitions can be taken even a step further. Perhaps the church can come to realize that though Christians may differ in matters of eschatological details, there are non-Christians, or "potential" brothers and sisters in Christ, who need and in many instances want the "integrity" or "fullness" of fellowship with Christ. Is it not incumbent on the Christian church to recast its eschatological debate, not to eliminate the discussion, but to change it from the obstacle it has become?

Arthur Glasser concludes his excellent three-part article, "Eschatology and Christianity's Future in the Middle East," by saying,

So then, let us not be caught up in any polarizing debate as to whether the State of Israel is a legitimate or illegitimate presence in the Middle East. In the mystery of God's providence it exists there! And its people, whether Jews or Arabs, need Christ. This being so, what higher priority can we have than to proclaim the Gospel to both peoples?[22]

If we make anything else a higher priority, then we risk failing the very people we have been debating about.

Stumbling Over the Right Block

The Bible tells us that nonbelievers, whether they are Jews, Muslims, or whoever, will stumble over the gospel and over the very identity of Christ. That, it seems, is inevitable if one is seriously considering whether Jesus is worthy to be followed. Indeed, from the Christian vantage point, it is not just inevitable; it is a necessary step toward true belief. All Christians reading these words can attest to the fact that, in some sense, before they gave their life to Him, they struggled and stumbled over whether Jesus was who He said He was. But if it is necessary to stumble over Christ, the crucial question is this: Will nonbelievers ever get to the right stumbling block, or will they have their legs taken out from under them before then by a different block? If they stumble over the church's emphasis on end-times prophecy, ethnicity, or the "Land," then they are stumbling over the wrong block.

The negative effects from the church's debate over eschatological details are quite powerful. When messianic Jews differ bitterly with Arab Christians, a rift is created among believers. When Christians shout mostly about who is entitled to the Land, an unnecessary rift is created between believers and nonbelievers. A mentality regarding those who are "in the club" and those who are excluded emerges. We see those nonbelievers (whether Jew or Arab) who we feel are not to be included as "them," while we remain "us." And in an "us-versus-them" paradigm, "they" are our enemy. Only after we come to realize that the gospel is the one truth worth dying for can we change our focus. We see that the gospel, though exclusive in its means, is inclusive in its saving scope. We no longer see "them" as our enemy to be vanquished but as people like we once were. They are missing something profound that we have found simply by God's grace. They are missing their Messiah. When we see "them" this way, we can then help them get past their stumbling blocks regarding land, ethnicity, and entitlement so that they can deal with the only stumbling block that truly matters—Jesus and His gospel.

Returning to the Question

So, how did I respond to the Palestinian man's question about the Middle East Conflict? I believe I responded in a way that Jesus would have responded, by asking him a question in return. I said to him, "Your question is important, and we'll get to it. But what I'm offering you first is evidence that Jesus rose from the dead after having died on the cross so you can be free from your sins. If that is true, then isn't there hope that your questions about Israel, love, and justice have an ultimate answer, even if we don't know what it is right now?"

He considered my question. "Yes," was his answer. And from there, our conversation was all about Jesus.

That kind of encounter is not new. Indeed, Jesus had a strikingly similar encounter with someone two thousand years ago in which He dealt with political and ethnic stumbling blocks that kept that person and an entire village from realizing ultimate truth. It is to that encounter we now turn.

Chapter 3

THE WAY AT THE WELL

Jesus and the Samaritan Woman

Conflict and suffering create opportunities. Seizing upon such opportunities sounds like an immoral thing. And indeed it can be. One does not need to look far or search too ardently to find those with significant power using a conflict and the resulting suffering to gain even more power and influence so that they may amass more wealth for themselves. But of course there are many instances in which conflict and suffering have been used as opportunities to exercise human compassion and show concern for the global welfare.

From conflict and suffering flow opportunities to provide medical aid for the sick, food for the hungry, and housing for the displaced. There are also opportunities to advance political views about the conflict, and there are opportunities to use such strife to advance an agenda or theory about how it should be handled. These opportunities are equally available to both the secular and religious worlds. To be sure, people from every perspective have taken advantage of such opportunities. Thus, whether seizing such opportunities is a negative or positive thing depends largely on one's motives.

Conflict and suffering provide Christians with opportunities to show the love of Christ by providing much-needed food and shelter. Christians can get involved politically to bring about positive change. Or, the church can use conflict to propagate a particular eschatological view about the end times. But we must be ever mindful not to pursue any one of these opportunities at the expense of the greatest opportunity presented to us by conflict and suffering. And this leads me to make a rather stark statement: The church must *take advantage* of conflict and suffering for Christ's sake.

The expression "taking advantage" may sound nefarious or opportunistic. And more often than not, we use the phrase to mean that the powerful stand upon the backs of the meek to further their own interests. "The rich *take advantage* of the poor," so we might hear someone say. But I would like to rescue that phrase from this dominant negative connotation. "Taking advantage" is, at its core, a neutral thing. And when it is done for Christ, it is not just morally acceptable for the Christian; it is morally incumbent upon the Christian.

But what do I mean by "taking advantage" of conflict and suffering for Christ's sake? I mean simply this: the feeling of sorrow, the desire for love, and the cry for justice that emerge from conflict and suffering have no meaningful resolution outside the Christian worldview. I will attempt to sustain that argument in this chapter and others. But if that is the case, then a Christian's taking advantage of conflict and suffering is not morally negative. Quite the contrary—it is the most moral thing a person can do.

What do I mean when I say it is morally incumbent on the Christian to take advantage of conflict and suffering? First, it is self-evident that one of the most valuable things a person can impart to one who is suffering is a real response to the sufferer's most deeply felt needs. Second, we find in the Gospels that Jesus did that very thing again and again, and every Christian should be committed to following His example.

Seeking a Samaritan

In the Gospel of John, we read of Jesus' encounter with a Samaritan woman that occurred very early in His earthly ministry. In context, Jesus was in Judea, encountering many different people, including the religious and social elite among the Jews. He had discussed and debated the nature of the gospel message and God's intentions for humanity. Having concluded His affairs among the religious and social elite for the time being, Jesus left for Galilee, a poorer region of Israel, where Jesus Himself had grown up. Providentially—and even poetically—the shortest route to Galilee was through an even more forsaken place, Samaria.

It was there in Samaria that one of the most profound personal encounters recorded in all the Bible takes place. Because the details are so important, I quote most of the Bible's account.

> He [Jesus] left Judea and departed again to Galilee. But He needed to go through Samaria.
>
> So He came to a city of Samaria which is called Sychar, near the plot of ground that Jacob gave to his son Joseph. Now Jacob's well was there. Jesus therefore, being wearied from His journey, sat thus by the well. It was about the sixth hour.
>
> A woman of Samaria came to draw water. Jesus said to her, "Give Me a drink." For His disciples had gone away into the city to buy food.
>
> Then the woman of Samaria said to Him, "How is it that You, being a Jew, ask a drink from me, a Samaritan woman?" For Jews have no dealings with Samaritans.
>
> Jesus answered and said to her, "If you knew the gift of God, and who it is who says to you, 'Give Me a drink,' you would have asked Him, and He would have given you living water."
>
> The woman said to Him, "Sir, You have nothing to

draw with, and the well is deep. Where then do You get that living water? Are You greater than our father Jacob, who gave us the well, and drank from it himself, as well as his sons and his livestock?"

Jesus answered and said to her, "Whoever drinks of this water will thirst again, but whoever drinks of the water that I shall give him will never thirst. But the water that I shall give him will become in him a fountain of water springing up into everlasting life."

The woman said to Him, "Sir, give me this water, that I may not thirst, nor come here to draw."

Jesus said to her, "Go, call your husband, and come here."

The woman answered and said, "I have no husband."

Jesus said to her, "You have well said, 'I have no husband,' for you have had five husbands, and the one whom you now have is not your husband; in that you spoke truly."

The woman said to Him, "Sir, I perceive that You are a prophet. Our fathers worshiped on this mountain, and you *Jews* say that in Jerusalem is the place where one ought to worship."

Jesus said to her, "Woman, believe Me, the hour is coming when you will neither on this mountain, nor in Jerusalem, worship the Father. You worship what you do not know; we know what we worship, for salvation is of the Jews. But the hour is coming, and now is, when the true worshipers will worship the Father in spirit and truth; for the Father is seeking such to worship Him. God is Spirit, and those who worship Him must worship in spirit and truth."

The woman said to Him, "I know that Messiah is coming" (who is called Christ). "When He comes, He will tell us all things."

Jesus said to her, "I who speak to you am He." (John 4:3–26)

This encounter is pregnant with details of how Jesus "took advantage" of the woman's suffering to show her the answers that only the gospel provides. He helped the Samaritan woman get past the sorrow of her past and present, her struggle with ethnic strife, her preoccupation with land entitlement, and ultimately her feeling of separation from God. In fact, in Jesus' encounter with the Samaritan woman, and later with the entire Samaritan village of Sychar, we find striking parallels to the issues in the Middle East Conflict and many other conflicts.

What are those parallels? The Samaritan woman brought to her encounter with Jesus her issues of sorrow, justice, and love. She expressed her sorrow over the rejection and marginalization that came not only from her ethnic background as a Samaritan, but also from her moral failings. In the exchange, we vividly see the sorrow that stemmed from her loss of dignity and self-respect. Cannot both the Arab and the Jew relate to the intense sorrow that accompanies the rejection of the outside community and the loss of so much that they hold dear? The woman also engaged with Jesus over the issues of entitlement to land, where God is to be worshiped, and the perception that she was spiritually inferior because of her race. The conflict between Jew and Arab is about nothing if it is not about competing ethnicities, spiritual privilege, and geographical entitlements. But the rank and file in the Holy Land, and those here and abroad, cry out for justice and a sense of equality. Finally, there was the woman's unmistakable need for love. She could not bear to be alone; she had lived with six different men, either in marriage or outside of it. Her need for love was so strong that she was willing to take up with just about any man who would throw a smile her way. The Jew, the Arab, in fact, everyone, yearns for that feeling of being loved, of being viewed as having intrinsic worth and value. As tragedy upon tragedy visits those directly or indirectly affected by conflict around the world, do we not hear their cry for a love that will somehow, someday rescue them from their agony?

Sorrow Unmasked

The Samaritan woman's sorrow is revealed more from the context leading up to her solitary encounter with Jesus than in the actual words she spoke. The Samaritan woman came to the well alone. History tells us that in those days, women did not venture out alone to collect water or food. The dangers were too great to risk going out alone, even in the day. Common decorum also dictated that women travel in groups or with their husbands. The women of the village likely would have had a daily scheduled time when they would all come to the well together to draw water. Yet at the well, the Samaritan woman was alone.

At the well, the woman encountered a man, a Jewish man, which likely caused her to feel an acute sense of condemnation. Her solitude was unusual and could mean only one thing. She was an outcast. As a Samaritan, she was considered a "half-breed" and therefore unclean by the Jews. As a woman with a checkered sexual past, she was considered unclean among the Samaritans. Thus, both those outside her ethnic sphere and those within her own ethnic sphere shunned her. She was, in a very real sense, a woman with no community. She was a peninsula that jutted out into a lake of rejection.

As she approached the well, the weight of Jesus' presence there must have been heavy for her to bear. But Jesus surprised her. Instead of walking away with disdain, He engaged her in conversation. He asked her for a drink from the well. Stunned, she retorted, "How is it that you, being a Jew, ask a drink from me, a Samaritan woman?" (John 4:9). Some have said her response had an instigating tone that subtly accused Jesus of being a racist simply because He was Jewish. Others have suggested that her response came from pure surprise and was just the first remark to come to her mind. I believe there is truth to both views. We will examine her accusations later, but now we will focus on the exchange that follows her surprise.

No doubt Jesus already had perceived from the circumstances that the woman was a social outcast. He knew why she was alone. But in their exchange, He offered her "living water," a gift that symbolized God's favor and salvation. Perhaps incredulously, but still with a sense of hope, she asked Him for the living water. "Sir, give me this water, that I may not thirst," she said. But she completed her request with a most important and telling statement, *"nor come here to draw"* (John 4:15).

The walk to the well was likely far for her. But I do not think she sought the "living water" so that she could get out of taking a long walk. Had that been her reason, she could have stopped at simply asking for the water so that she would not thirst. No, there was something more, something sorrowful, about her coming to the well to draw every day. She came alone. Every day, when other women came to the well with their husbands or with other women to draw water, she came in solitude. Every long trip to that well was a reminder of her station in life. Every trip served as a constant reminder of her rejection, her loss, and her sorrow. Perhaps she had a glimmer of hope that Jesus could at least take that daily reminder of her sorrow from her. Perhaps that is why she implicitly asked if Jesus could remove the burden from her.

Jesus picked up on the statement and actually forced her to explicitly confront the issue. "Go, call your husband, and come here," He said. As we see in the dialogue, Jesus already knew that she had no husband. He knew that she had had five husbands and was living with a sixth man who was not her husband. In this, Jesus forced her to do what she unconsciously wanted to do herself: confront the very source of her sorrow. Her sorrow, her shame, must be exposed. Only then could it be dealt with. Only then could Jesus show her that God saw her sorrow, that He heard her cry, and that He cared.

He showed this by speaking with her. She did not expect that. She expected rejection and derision. Simply, she expected more loss and thus more sorrow. But He *spoke* to her. He looked her in the eye. He forced her to confront her own sin and the sorrow of loss that resulted so that He could show her what she could receive. She had spent much of her life in a state of loss. She had lost marriages. She had lost dignity. She had lost community. She had lost self-respect. Jesus offered her something far more valuable than what she had lost. He offered her communion with God. He offered her God's respect. He offered her a place in His kingdom. Though in her lifetime the losses would not be undone, they could be healed.

Sorrow that is borne of loss is the hallmark of the Middle East Conflict. Many Arabs in Palestine, Lebanon, and Iraq can attest to the bottomless sorrow that forms from the intensity of their losses. Many Jews in Israel join in that tragic fraternity of pain. The bombing of Qana in Lebanon, where so many children died, and the deadly explosions in Israeli shopping malls serve as exclamation points to the wailings from those sorrowful many. They have suffered at the hands of others, and they have suffered loss by their own hands. But the sorrow of loss bleeds out beyond the Middle East's borders. The many thousands who live abroad in Europe and America and even Asia feel the agony of loss. Their relatives and friends suffer, so they suffer. Their homeland is torn apart, and so they are torn apart. But like the Samaritan woman of Sychar, no one's hands are clean. And thus, like her, we all must face the loss and the shame that come from the sorrow we have inflicted and that has been inflicted on us.

Jesus offers us something to ease that sorrow. He offers us Himself and His righteousness. As He did with the Samaritan woman, He offers us the communion with one who Himself knows what it means to suffer. He offers us the cosmic shoulder upon which to shed tears. He offers us the hope that, though in this world we have trouble, we can take heart because Jesus, the Author of life and the Master over death, has overcome the world (John 16:33). Shortly, we shall see the details of how Jesus has provided that hope.

A Cry for Justice

A major facet of the Middle East Conflict is a preoccupation with who, by virtue of their DNA, has the right to recognized nationhood or to be considered God's chosen. The history of the Jews is one marked by prosperity and promises, but also by great tragedy and persecution. This persecution had its most vicious expression in the Third Reich's "final solution"—the attempted genocide of the Jews. That persecution stemmed from the monstrous belief that Jews, by virtue of their DNA, are inferior to those of other races or ethnicities. *Ironic* is almost too anemic a word to describe how those chosen by God through the ancient revelations repeatedly have been seen as ethnically inferior and good only for the gas chamber.

But Jews do not have a grotesque monopoly on the charge of being inferior. Africans, Indians, and Arabs have shared the sting of that evil. Perhaps too numerous to recount are the stories of Palestinians being ousted from the land of their birth by Jewish settlers who based their right to confiscate the Palestinians' homes on the mere fact that they were Jewish. Gary M. Burge relates the stories of Palestinian families who lost their homes to Jewish families following the 1948 conflict and the 1967 war. One Arab man was told by Jewish officials that he would be paid only a token price for his home as "watchman's wages" because he was an Arab and the Palestinians had merely been serving as watchmen over the Jews' property for two thousand years.[1] Indeed, the deep sting of racism and ethnic intimidation has been and continues to be felt by both Jews and Arabs alike.

I cannot help but recall an episode as a young boy when I was educated on this cruel reality of our fallen world. When I was only eleven years old, my younger brother, my cousin, and I had gone to a local pizza shop for a slice of pizza on a warm summer afternoon. After we received our slices, we went outside the establishment to enjoy our food and the weather. We were standing just outside the pizza shop's windows when I looked into the shop past my own reflection. What I saw shocked me. One of the employees, a young man about eighteen years of age, was making a very profane gesture at me. Strangely, and perhaps because I was so shocked, I walked in and asked him if he meant that gesture for me.

"That's right, camel jockey," he answered me. "What are you going to do about it?"

My shock at the gesture was suddenly dwarfed by my shock at the ethnic assault. This person did not know me, yet he was perfectly willing to make me feel as though I was worthy of his contempt simply because of my ethnicity. He had unjustly tried to rob me of my dignity. It was my first education in the kind of pain that the injustice of racism can inflict. It was a lesson and a feeling I have never forgotten.

The ancient proverb says that there is nothing new under the sun (Eccl. 1:9). Two thousand years ago, when Jesus encountered the Samaritan woman at Jacob's well, the injustice that stems from ethnic claims to superiority was prevalent as well. After Jesus had asked her for a drink from the well, the woman asked, "How is it that You, being a Jew, ask a drink from me, a Samaritan woman?" (John 4:9). The narrative provides the important historical fact that she said this because "Jews have no dealings with Samaritans."

It is interesting that one of the first things out of this woman's mouth was this question. In the first century culture, one might expect the woman to be diminutive or timid in conversing with this Jewish man, especially in light of what society considered to be her lower moral standing. It seems likely that in that culture, she would have just fulfilled His request without really looking Him in the eye, gotten herself some water, and then left. But she defied expectations with her boldness and directness. Although her question may have been prompted by sheer surprise, there is a possibility that she was also being defiant. Whatever the case may be, it is clear that she was unexpectedly bold. Her personality can account for part of it, but I think the context of the passage gives us more insight.

The woman's first question speaks volumes about the reason for her attitude. She asked a question and made a statement at the same time. Such questions are usually more accusatory than interrogatory. The rejection she had felt from Jews because of her ethnicity had left its mark on her psyche. So prominent was the mark and so deep the scar that the first thing she thought to say to this Jewish man was accusatory.

Being judged based on one's race or ethnicity is one of the worst forms of injustice a person can suffer. Anyone who has been the object of scorn or ridicule (or perhaps even worse, indifference) because of his or her race develops a sensitivity that is so deep that it dominates and practically becomes the person's identity. Race and ethnicity are immutable characteristics that we cannot change. Further, they are neutral characteristics that have no moral significance. Thus, to judge someone on such bases is the height of arbitrary and capricious judgment. When we are judged based on something about us that is morally neutral and that we cannot change—and that need not be changed—our very right to exist is called into question and demeaned. As a result, we can become so preoccupied with defending against the attack on our identity that defensiveness *becomes* our identity. Every encounter we have with those of another ethnicity or race is seen only in terms of that strife. And in the end, the assault on our identity is successful if we no longer know who we are in God's eyes. There can be no greater robbery than that.

The Samaritan woman had dealt with that strife her entire life. She was, as history tells us, a half-breed, a mix of Jewish blood and Gentile blood.[2] The tension between Jews and Samaritans was so bitter and intense that Roman intervention was sometimes necessary.[3]

Among the many areas of brokenness in her life, the ethnic tension seems to have been a particularly sensitive one. Perhaps this explains both the content of her first statement to Jesus and its boldness. In fact, her second question to Jesus still focused on ethnic strife and on her defensiveness about her own identity (John 4:12). In response to her accusation-in-the-form-of-a-question about Jewish superiority, Jesus pointed to His identity as the "gift of God" (John 4:10).

This was a completely audacious claim to make to a perfect stranger in a hostile territory. The woman responded to Jesus' claim with incredulity. Perhaps she even took exception to the fact that Jesus seemed to ignore her statement about her own identity and instead focused on His own. "Are *You* greater than *our* father Jacob, who gave *us* the well, and drank from it himself?" she asked (John 4:12).

Jesus' answer showcases that His intention was not to deal with her issues about *ethnic* identity and the injustice she has experienced because of it, but to offer her a spiritual identity through her recognition of His true identity. "Whoever drinks of the water that I shall give him will never thirst," said Jesus. "But the water that I shall give him will become in him a fountain of water springing up into everlasting life" (John 4:14).

Though she eventually came to understand Jesus' messianic role later in their exchange, her focus at this point remained on the issue of ethnicity and even geographical entitlement. "*Our* fathers worshiped on this mountain, and *you Jews* say that in Jerusalem is the place where one ought to worship" (John 4:20). The mountain she referred to was Mount Gerizim, which was the Samaritans' holy site, as opposed to the Jews' holy site, the temple in Jerusalem. One can easily imagine her making a gesture toward Gerizim while making this statement, as the mountain was in plain view from Jacob's well. In making this statement, she actually made two indictments. First, she pointed out the ethnic strife between the Jews and Samaritans. Second, she pointed out the geographical strife born from that ethnic strife. Around one hundred fifty years prior to her conversation with Jesus, the Jews had obliterated the Samaritans' temple on Mount Gerizim. In turn, the Samaritans had tried to deface and defile the Jewish temple. But the ruined temple of Gerizim, where the Samaritan holy temple once stood, was in sight of Jesus and the Samaritan

woman and likely became the elephant in the room during
their exchange. The wounds of racial injustice and rejection
were visible both figuratively and literally.

Yet again, however, Jesus would not take the bait and quib-
ble about physicality and geography. But He did not ignore
her wounds. He dealt with her own feeling of self-superiority
toward the Jews, which stemmed from her victim mentality.
Jesus conspicuously pointed out to her that "salvation is of the
Jews" (John 4:22). Often in His personal encounters, Jesus
would say something to get people thinking a little deeper
about their own assumptions. He would give them the prover-
bial "stone in the shoe" to get them thinking and keep them
thinking.

He did exactly that in Luke 10:25–37, when confronted
by someone who was the polar opposite of the Samaritan
woman—a self-righteous teacher of the Law. That man, seeking to test Jesus, asked what he must do to have eternal life.
The answer was to love God and love his neighbor as himself.
The teacher of the Law pressed on with the question, "And
who is my neighbor?" Jesus answered with the parable of the
Good Samaritan. He juxtaposed the self-righteous attitude
of religious Jews against the self-giving attitude of a good
Samaritan. Jesus purposefully used a Samaritan as an example of true neighborliness to bring about a visceral reaction
in the Jews listening so that he could illustrate that godly love
does not respect DNA and is truly just.

With the same technique, Jesus helped the Samaritan
woman at the well to open up about her racial issues. In so
doing, Jesus exposed the fact that racial relations issues were
more important to this woman than ultimate spiritual truth.
In other words, Jesus pointed out to her, and points out to us
today, that the victim of racial marginalization runs the risk
of making ethnicity the dominant issue in life at the expense of
all other concerns. And in so doing, the victim has unwittingly
helped the victimizer keep that which is most profound from
the victim's consciousness—her intrinsic value, regardless of

ethnicity, before God. With the woman at Jacob's well, Jesus quickly but effectively exposed her stumbling block so that she could willingly walk around it.

But Jesus did not leave the stumbling block looming there for her. Instead, Jesus offered satisfaction for her longing for justice and equal treatment. He pointed out to her that "salvation is of the Jews," so that she would understand the particular place that Jews have in God's purposes. But in the same breath, Jesus *included her* along with the Jews as among those who can have the salvation of the Lord.

> Jesus said to her, "Woman, believe Me, the hour is coming when *you* will neither on this mountain, nor in Jerusalem, worship the Father. . . . But the hour is coming, and now is, when the *true worshipers* will worship the Father in spirit and truth; for the Father is seeking such to worship Him. God *is* Spirit, and those who worship Him must worship in spirit and truth." (John 4:21–24, emphasis added)

In saying that "salvation is of the Jews," Jesus points out a theological fact. But that fact does not mean that Jews, by virtue of their DNA, are somehow saved or exempt from God's righteous judgment. To say that would be to nullify Jesus' next statement, that true worshipers are those who worship in spirit and truth. There is nothing in one's particular physicality that puts one in good stead with God. Rather, as we truly grasp the person of Christ, a transformation of our spirit reconciles our relationship to God.

Indeed, Jesus' statement that "salvation is of the Jews" actually emphasized the spiritual and gracious aspects of God's interaction with humanity. God chose in His providence to use a lowly nation, an unremarkable and despised people, to bring His message to the world. Ultimately, the embodiment of God's interaction with humanity is found in the incarnation of God in Christ—Jesus the Jew from the marginal town of

Nazareth. Jesus told the marginalized Samaritan woman that she too could be a true worshiper in spirit and truth, whose worship did not depend on land and location. How wonderful for her to hear that the seemingly lowly in this world are part of the otherworldly kingdom of God.

Jesus told the Samaritan woman that ethnicity is not ultimately important to God. Jesus told her that geography is unimportant to God. He told her that her spirit, that which makes her a child of God, is what is important. Her entire life, people had treated her unjustly because of her DNA, and she had responded in kind. Her whole life, people had tried to steal away her dignity by focusing on her physicality, and she had focused on it herself. But Jesus told her that God in His perfect justice offers membership in the kingdom to everyone, regardless of ethnicity or geography. Through His interaction with the woman at the well, Jesus tells us that the identity that bears the stamp of equality is not the identity borne of ethnicity, but the identity that bears the *imago Dei*—the image of God.

If the unsanctified corporeal matter is not what is of concern to God, how much less then is the dirt of the earth and the artificial walls of man-made temples? But the profound paradox that Jesus gave the woman is that the true temple, the true sacred ground, is the temple of the individual's body, where the *imago Dei* finds its place and the Spirit of Christ dwells. The paradox lies in the fact that while God disregards the differences in ethnic genetic codes, He exalts each believer's body. Through Christ, the body that was of no regard and the physical that seemed so banal are transformed into the true temple of the living God. As Ravi Zacharias has written,

> *We* are His temple. We do not turn in a certain direction to pray. We are not bound by having to go into a building so that we can commune with God. There are no unique postures and times and limitations that restrict our access to God. My relationship with God is intimate and

personal. The Christian does not go to the temple to worship. The Christian takes the temple with him or her.[4]

Today, Jews look down on Arabs, and Arabs look down on
Jews. What may have started as a territorial conflict has now
become a racial conflict. Some may not share in that assess-
ment and may strongly disagree. But I have heard Jews in
conversation about Arabs, and I have heard Arabs in conversation about Jews. The present conflict is nothing if it is not
racially motivated. The ethnic claims have branched out into
claims about land entitlement. Aided by Christian interpreta-
tions, Arabs and Jews sharply divide over geographical issues.
Both proclaim entitlement to the land called Israel. Both Jews
and Muslims lay claim to the particular plot of land called the
Temple Mount by Jews and the Al-Aqsa Mosque by Muslims.
As a result of these ethnic claims and these land-related
claims, injustice upon injustice has been wrought.

Of course, the wrongs each side has wrought on the other
should not be ignored, and the need to resolve the right to certain
land must be addressed. But our attempts to bring about a just
solution stem from an obsession with the corporeal—ethnicity
and real estate. We speak only about what borders each nation
should have and what Jews and Arabs are entitled to. Like the
Samaritan woman, our desire for justice and equality focuses
almost entirely on land and ethnicity.

Through His encounter with that Samaritan woman, however, Jesus shows us that such preoccupations are spiritually
unhealthy and ultimately destructive. Jesus tells us that we
must first be obsessed or preoccupied with that which is non-
corporeal. We must be focused on the spirit and the truth.
Jesus showed that true equality begins first with the realization that we are all in equal need of one thing, and that is
spiritual communion with God.

Two thousand years after Jesus' meeting with the Samaritan
woman, I found myself in dialog with the young Palestinian
man I mentioned in the previous chapter. Like the Samaritan

woman, he was preoccupied with ethnicity and geography. I had taken a lesson from Jesus in how to respond. I did not ignore his important question, but I focused on the fundamental gift that is equally available to Palestinians and Jews alike. I focused on Jesus, His crucifixion, and His resurrection. I focused on the truth of the gospel and how it provides true resolution to the quest for justice. If this angry Palestinian would truly embrace Jesus as the Samaritan did, he would see Jews and everyone else in a different light. He would see nonbelieving Jews as those who need the gospel as He once did. Likewise, if Jews would embrace Jesus as their Messiah, they would look at nonbelieving Arabs as those who need that Messiah. The transformation is intoxicating to think of. Arabs and Jews, who were once so bent on taking from each other, would be changed into people who are obsessed with sharing that which makes them truly equal.

A Need for Love

The Samaritan woman's life illustrates the tragedy that ensues when the natural human desire for meaningful love goes unfulfilled and even abused. The lack of fulfillment comes not just from without but also from within. At times, a person's unfulfilled desire for love can be taken advantage of and used as the means to satisfy another person's baser instincts. At other times, our perceptions of what it means to be loved become skewed so that we equate being alone with being lonely and being single with being unloved. The tragedy in such a situation is that in our desire to be free from loneliness, we cannot stand to be alone, and we repeatedly find ourselves in destructive relationships with just about anyone who smiles at us.

Though there is no way to know this with certainty from the Scriptures, there is good reason to believe that the Samaritan woman was the victim of her own distorted perception of love and of the abuse of others who took advantage of her perceptions. In their exchange, Jesus brought this up in a most obvious way. After telling her that He could offer her "living water," she asked for it so that she would not have to come to the well to draw. Jesus responded with what seems like an out-of-place statement: "Go, call your husband, and come here," He said to her (John 4:16).

Exposed, she has no choice but to respond, "I have no husband."

Jesus would not leave the matter at that and exposed her even more. "You have well said, 'I have no husband,'" He said, "for you have had five husbands, and the one whom you now have is not your husband; in that you spoke truly" (John 4:17–18). Interestingly, He pointed out that in saying she had no husband, she "spoke truly." Until that moment, she had been playing coy with Him. Although she may have stated non-false propositions or opinions, nothing was actually a matter of ultimate truth to her. In saying that she had no husband, she spoke truly; but she left out the important details that explained her situation in life.

But why did Jesus ask her to bring her husband? I believe there are at least two reasons. First, the woman had engaged in their conversation with something of a self-righteous tone. In some sense, Jesus had had enough of her banter and was now poised to get to the heart of the matter with her. He had to convince her of her own sin in order to reveal Himself as the Redeemer that she could accept.

But there is another reason. She had fallen into a life of sin and rejection because her natural desire for love and acceptance had been twisted, and she had been complicit in that twisting. Remember, she came to the well alone, with no husband and not in the company of other women, as was the custom and practice. She came without a husband because the relationship she now had was adulterous in some fashion. She came without other women because her moral shortcomings had caused her to be ostracized among her own people. Her deep desire for a fulfilling love had become twisted and had resulted in her rejection. The irony, of course, is that her efforts to find love through morally questionable means led to a life of loneliness in which true love was the farthest thing from her. No man had truly loved her. Her own people did not truly love her. And she had not truly loved anyone. The result was brokenness.

Having been required to come clean, she finally acknowledged Jesus' special stature, calling Him a prophet. She had taken one more step toward actually listening to Jesus. One can almost hear the expectant tone in her voice when she said to Him, "'I know that Messiah is coming. . . . When He comes, He will tell us all things'" (John 4:25). All that preceded this statement was Jesus' winsomeness and His prophetic ability to reveal her innermost being. Other than that, there was nothing to prompt her to mention the Messiah. After all, there were many prophets who were not the Messiah. But having encountered Jesus in this intensely personal way, she saw something that caused her heart and mind to leap at the possibility that He could be the long-awaited Promised One. Perhaps she longed to know if He was the Messiah because, if it were true, she would finally find a pure and holy fulfillment of her lifelong search for love.

And then with remarkable directness, Jesus told her the words that undid her last bit of resistance: "I who speak to you am He" (John 4:26).

It is remarkable that to so many others, who placed confidence in their heritage and their own righteousness, Jesus spoke of His identity in parables or by references to Old Testament prophecies. But to this broken, lonely, victimized Samaritan woman, who had finally come to the point that she wanted to know the truth, He was startlingly direct.[5] He gave her no parable, no cryptic response, and no reference to an Old Testament prophecy about His identity. He disclosed Himself to her cleanly. And in doing that, He told her that her desire for love had finally found its intended object. God had known her desire for holy relationship because He had instilled it in

her very nature. Now, God incarnate had come in the person
of Jesus, so that she could truly relate to Him. But more than
that, He had come so that He could later lay down His life for
her sin and pay her penalty when she could not pay it herself.
God in Christ, standing before her at Jacob's well, had offered
her that which she wanted so much that she was willing to
destroy her own life to get it. Jesus so passionately wanted her
to feel truly loved that He was willing to lay down His life. He
showed her that He is the Messiah. He is God. He is the lover
of her soul.

Having her sorrow dealt with, her injustice righted, and
her desire for love finally fulfilled, the Samaritan woman put
aside the conflict that had ruled her life for so long and allowed
Jesus to rule it instead. In the simplest terms, she believed
and was filled.

In the midst of the pain of conflict comes the cry, "Does God
love me?" It is a natural and understandable question when it
comes from one who has suffered so much. Those parents who
lost their children in Qana, those parents whose children are
killed in the Israeli Defense Force, and those who lost loved
ones on September 11 ask this same question with bitter tears.
Indeed, I have read and heard Jews lament that no loving God
would have allowed the Holocaust to occur. Many books have
been written in answer to such objections, so I will not go into
a detailed response here.[6] But for our purposes, we see that
Jesus did not skirt the issue of suffering in dealing with the
Samaritan woman. He provided her with the reality that indeed God did love her, though others did not, and that His love
would carry her through this life. He provided her with the
hope of eternal fulfillment in the hereafter.

Only one worldview offers Jews, Arabs, and everyone who
has felt unloved an assurance that though the world may not
offer love, God certainly does. The charge has long been that
if an all-powerful, loving God exists, He would do something
to offer us hope. Only in the person of Christ do we see that
what God offers is an inclusive invitation to be part of the fam-

ily of God. Later, we will see that though the invitation is inclusive, the means by which God lovingly offers that hope are exclusive.

A Wildfire in Samaria

A truly remarkable aspect of Jesus' encounter with the woman at Jacob's Well lies in its aftermath. The apostle John tells us that almost immediately after Jesus disclosed to her that He was the Messiah, the woman hurriedly left to tell the rest of her Samaritan village of Sychar that she had met the one and only Christ. Notice how the narrative says that after Jesus disclosed to her that He was the Messiah, His disciples returned, having retrieved food. But about the woman, John says, *"The woman then left her waterpot,* went her way into the city, and said to the men, 'Come, see a Man who told me all things that I ever did. Could this be the Christ?'" (John 4:28–29, emphasis added). She had come to the well to draw water, but she was so spiritually charged that she left her water pot—the very thing she came there to fill—to tell the people of Sychar about what had truly filled her soul.

Remember, this woman was an outcast among her own people. They would have nothing to do with her. Yet she went immediately to tell the men of her village about her encounter with Jesus. She was no longer ashamed of her past. Only the monumental truth that came from her meeting with Jesus mattered. Her lowly position with the Samaritans would not stop her. Her people simply must know that the Messiah had come. They must be redeemed. Their sorrow could be lifted. Their desire for justice could be satisfied. Their need for love could be fulfilled.

From a worldly standpoint, she owed her fellow villagers nothing. They had treated her with contempt. They had judged her. She easily could have kept Jesus' disclosure to herself. Jesus did not command her to tell them who He was, but He had freed her. She was no longer a slave to sin. She was no longer a slave to racism. She was no longer a slave to politics. She was now one who worshiped in spirit and in truth. Her spiritual response to that transformation could not be contained. The compulsion was to spread the news about the one who offered living water.

Samaritans hated Jews, and Jews hated Samaritans. Yet, the woman ran to bid the Samaritans of Sychar to go see a Jewish man who had given significance to her life. What kind of conviction was in her voice? What fire was in her eyes? Though we cannot be certain, we can imagine that her voice was intense and her eyes were ablaze, for the Samaritans of Sychar *listened to her and responded.*

The narrative tells us that the Samaritans of Sychar "went out of the city and came to Him" (John 4:30). They did not dismiss the woman's report. They responded. There must have been something new in her that stirred them to act. Indeed, we read that many of the Samaritans believed in Jesus because of the woman's testimony (John 4:39). But these spiritually starving Samaritans were not satisfied with only a vicarious experience with the Messiah. They desired their own personal encounter with this Jesus. Thus, they came to Jesus and asked Him to stay with them, which He did for two days. Though many had believed in Him because of the woman's testimony, many more came to believe in Him because of their own intimate encounter with Him. The Samaritans had invited a Jew to stay with them, and He had accepted. While they broke bread at supper with a Jewish man, they also communed with God incarnate.

And they were never the same. After Jesus had stayed with them, the Samaritans of Sychar, the same people that shunned the woman for years, returned to her in gratitude. They said to her, "It is no longer because of what you said that we believe, for we have heard for ourselves and know that this One is indeed the Savior of the world" (John 4:42 NASB). He was not the Savior of the Samaritans. He was not the Savior of the Jews. *He was the Savior of the world.* Salvation had spread in

Sychar like a wildfire, and sorrow was no more. Justice was satisfied because all were included in God's redemptive plan, and love was enjoyed because at last it was truly given and truly received.

Not Leaving "Well Enough" Alone

Jesus' plan in engaging the woman at the well was not for her benefit only. He orchestrated their encounter, fully intending for His truth to spread in that community. We know this from what He told His disciples as the woman was spreading the news and urging the Samaritans to come and see Jesus.

Jesus' disciples had gone to retrieve food and left Him at the well. When they returned to the well, the woman left. The Scripture is careful to point out that they did not ask Jesus about His encounter with the woman (John 4:27). Instead, they simply urged Jesus to have lunch (John 4:31). But Jesus responded that He had been satiating Himself with the Samaritan woman's salvation and would soon be dining on the fruits of the salvation of her entire village. The apostle John gives it to us this way:

> Jesus said to them, "My food is to do the will of Him who sent Me, and to finish His work. Do you not say, 'There are still four months and then comes the harvest'? Behold, I say to you, lift up your eyes and look at the fields, for they are already white for harvest! And he who reaps receives wages, and gathers fruit for eternal life, that both he who sows and he who reaps may rejoice together. For in this the saying is true: 'One sows and another reaps.' I sent you to reap that for which you have not labored; others have labored, and you have entered into their labors." (John 4:34–38)

At this point, the woman had just left Jesus. But He was aware that their conversation would effect the spread of the gospel in her village. In fact, He intended that very effect. He was not satisfied with the salvation and resolution of sorrow, justice, and love that occurred at the well. It was simply not enough. By telling His disciples to lift up their eyes and look at the fields that were "white for harvest," Jesus was telling them—and He is telling us today—that every encounter where His gospel finds good soil will be used by God to bring about redemption in individuals and also in whole communities. Each time we push past the obstacles of race and land entitlement and instead share Jesus with someone, we unleash the power of God to create in that person an evangelist who will bring hope to others. If that is the case, then there is no greater commission and service to the world that the Church can undertake than to preach the gospel of Jesus Christ to a world in conflict.

Uniqueness Illustrated

Jesus' discussion with the Samaritan woman at Jacob's well was not the first time that God met someone by a well to relieve that person's burdens. In Genesis 16, we read that God encountered Hagar, the mother of Ishmael, at a well during one of her darkest times. Hagar was the Egyptian handmaiden of Abraham's wife, Sarah. Sarah had offered Hagar to Abraham to bear him a son because Sarah was barren. Many consider Ishmael, the son Hagar bore to Abraham, to be the progenitor of the Arabs and, eventually, the Muslims. In Genesis 16:7–9, we find Hagar, pregnant with Ishmael but in utter despair after having been forced out of the community by Sarah. Hagar had suffered what seemed to be an injustice. Although she carried Abraham's firstborn son, she had been marginalized. Hagar had been cast out, severed from her relationship with Abraham, her most intimate relationship on earth. The injustice and apparent lack of love resulted in her sorrow. But her suffering provided God the opportunity to reveal to this woman, the mother of the Arabs, that God was in command of

her destiny and that He could resolve the issues arising from
her suffering.

God comforted Hagar with the news that He had plans for
her son, Ishmael. His plans were to make Ishmael and his prog-
eny free and numerous. God ordered Hagar's steps and forever
changed her destiny from sorrow, injustice, and loneliness to
rejoicing, purpose, and covenant with God. Ultimately, all these
things will be fulfilled for her, her son, and their descendants in
the person of God's own Son, Jesus Christ. How remarkable it is
that in the very time when God was establishing His covenant
with the Hebrews through whom the Messiah would come, God
provided comfort and purpose to the Arabs as well.[7]

But how will this fulfillment come to pass? There is a growing movement in ecumenical circles to answer this by stressing
the commonality of ancestry of Jews, Arabs, and Christians
through Abraham. Jews and Arabs claim Abraham as their
genetic father. Christians claim him as their spiritual patri-
arch. To engender peace among the monotheistic faiths, ecu-
menicists ask, "Why should we be at odds when we are all one
family?" They declare, "We will stop fighting when we realize
we have the same father."

But the danger we run into looking to the commonality of
our origins is that we might focus on the beginning of God's
redemptive plan at the expense of embracing its fulfillment.
Looking to Abraham as our common father to foster understanding and peace is a noble idea. But I am compelled to say
that it is wrongheaded. History teaches, and indeed Jesus'
conversation with the Samaritan woman confirms, that the
bitterest feuds are family feuds. Jesus did not try to help the
Samaritan woman find peace by pointing to her common ancestry with Jews through Abraham. Jesus showed her and
shows us that resolution of sorrow, justice, and love does not
come from focusing on what we have in common but from focusing on the common thing we all lack. Peace does not come
from the fact that we have the same father. It comes only when
we realize that we can have the same Son.

That Son, the Son of God and Son of Man, is the only means by which true peace can be offered and received. But what is that peace? What does it mean, and how do we attain it? It is to these questions we now turn.

Chapter 4

WORLD PEACE

The Oldest Cliché in the Book

We cheer for that which scratches our itching ears. That is an old cliché that conveys a generally true proposition. Indeed, it is a cliché about the appeal of clichés. Profound sayings that once started as pithy ways to remember important truths or communicate our values get overused and eventually devolve into trite, almost meaningless statements. Yet at times we still smile and even cheer when we hear them.

A few years ago, I saw a film titled *Miss Congeniality*. It illustrates my point and highlights the meaningless yet enduring allure of clichés.[1] The premise of the film is that the FBI is trying to catch an unknown villain who is planning to perpetrate a crime during a national beauty pageant. To flush out the villain, a female FBI agent goes undercover as a contestant in the beauty pageant. Unfortunately, her domineering and gruff demeanor is far from what we have come to think of as the quintessential beauty queen, making her transformation to pageant contestant difficult and comical. She fumbles her way through the contests' many stages, especially the stereotypical "current events" question, which is meant to gauge the contestants' compassion and consideration for the world's ills. At first, we are not given the emcee's question, only rapid cuts to the contestants' answers. Over and over again, each contestant answers, "World peace," as if chanting a mantra. And each time, as if hearing the answer for the first time, the audience erupts in applause. Finally when it is the undercover FBI agent's turn, we hear the question: "What is the one most important thing our society needs?"

"Tougher sentencing for parole violators, Stan," the undercover agent answers without hesitation.

The audience is silent. Sensing her flub, the agent corrects herself. "And . . . world peace!" And the audience erupts in cheers.

The scene is humorous because it pokes fun at both the contestants and the audience. The contestants unthinkingly mouth the lofty idea of "world peace." Not to be outdone in terms of superficiality, the audience mindlessly cheers each time. The contestants spit out a well-meaning cliché, and the audience is eager to eat it up. Of course, everyone wants the elusive "world peace," but when the FBI agent unexpectedly suggests a specific step toward achieving that goal, the eagerness dies. This reflects a certain reality that we all experience. We cheer for well-meaning, good-sounding ideals, but we balk when we are offered something of substance that may actually require us to think critically and take a stand to realize that ideal. The sentiment rather than the solution is what makes us stand up and cheer.

This illustration is not just about the general proposition that we embrace clichés while eschewing substance. It shows how history's most desired goal—world peace—has degraded into a mere colloquialism and even a punch line. World peace is now an empty cliché for two reasons. First, the concept is so vague and lofty that it is difficult to see how it can be achieved in any real way. Second, the phrase has become so overused that the words are now just sounds that fill the silence or provide the appearance of sincerity for politicians and inspirational speakers. Making a toast to "world peace" at parties has become as meaningless as asking someone "How are you?" when greeting them. No one actually expects anything of substance to follow either phrase.

But how has this happened? How have we come to the point where the most strived-for goal in human history has become a cosmic punch line? Have we ceased to care for the welfare of civilization, or is it that we have just lost faith in the concept of world peace but hang on to the notion for sentimental reasons? I believe we still want world peace, but it remains missing for at least two reasons.

First, we have come to view world peace as impossible because we see it as achievable only through human effort. And we have good reason to have little faith in human effort. Both history and current world events show us that even where people have achieved great successes in bringing peace to war-torn regions, humanity still finds some way to either recreate the rift that caused the original strife or find a new grievance to justify violence. When the sapling of enmity is cut down, if it does not regrow in that same spot, it will spring up in some other area of the world. We appear to have extinguished the hostility in Northern Ireland, but the conflict in Rwanda flared up. We appear to have stamped out the scourge of apartheid in South Africa, but the injustices in the Middle East have lived on. We halted the Third Reich's genocidal surge, but in Eastern Europe, ethnic cleansing marched on. Through human effort, we have sought to establish peace in our time, but again and again we are disappointed until we succumb to a feeling of helplessness.

The second reason we have lost hope for world peace is related to the first. We have forgotten the divine rather than human origin of the desire for world peace. World peace has become such a prevalent cliché and empty notion because we have divorced the concept from the context of the phrase's apparent origin. That contextual origin centers on one of the most profound moments in human history, which took place two thousand years ago on the first Christmas.

The Birth of Peace

The New Testament narrates Jesus' birth to an obscure family in an obscure town in an obscure eastern Roman province. The account is well known, of course. Mary, a young virgin who was betrothed to a good man named Joseph, gave birth to a baby boy in a stable and made an animal's feeding trough the baby's first bed. In Luke 2 a part of the story is told from the perspective of average shepherds who were far away from the new, young family in the stable. The narrative begins with a tranquil scene as shepherds watched over their flocks in the still and quiet of the night. We can imagine a breeze across the fields providing the background noise that was occasionally accompanied by the low bleating of sheep.

Suddenly the dark stillness was instantly changed into a blinding radiance and cacophony of praise. The angel of the Lord suddenly appeared to the unsuspecting shepherds and announced the birth of the Messiah. The glory of the Lord shone all around the shepherds. The mind-boggling intensity of the experience compared with the previous quiet and dark caused the shepherds to become terrified, or, as the King James translation puts it, they were "sore afraid."

> And there were in the same country shepherds abiding in the field, keeping watch over their flock by night. And, lo, the angel of the Lord came upon them, and the glory of the Lord shone round about them: and they were sore afraid. And the angel said unto them, Fear not: for, behold, I bring you good tidings of great joy, which shall be to all people. For unto you is born this day in the city of David a Saviour, which is Christ the Lord. And this shall be a sign unto you; Ye shall find the babe wrapped in swaddling clothes, lying in a manger. (Luke 2:8–12 KJV)

The shepherds' wits were given no reprieve as the intensity of the scene only increased.

> And suddenly there was with the angel a multitude of the
> heavenly host praising God, and saying, Glory to God in
> the highest, and *on earth peace*, good will toward men.
> (Luke 2:13–14 KJV, emphasis added)

Think of the radiance, the immensity of such a sight. We have
become accustomed to thinking of this account as something
out of a children's Christmas pageant, the angels having diminutive voices and floppy paper wings, and the audience saying
"aaww" at the cute parts. But the reality of the experience was
far more powerful. Thousands of heavenly angels filled the sky
around the shepherds and their flock. Such a sight distorted
all sense of perspective and scale. The multitude, in one voice,
boomed praise to the Lord. In unison the heavenly multitude
proclaimed in the grandest fashion imaginable that the Messiah
had been born. The sentiment that has now become the mother
of all clichés—uttered only in superficial contests of outward
beauty and in the occasional Christmas carol—was announced
by a beautiful chorus of heavenly angels whose jubilant praise
would drown out the whooping and cheering of any crowd.

The angels expressly connected the concept of world peace
with the birth of Jesus of Nazareth, the one who would claim
to be God's Messiah and would prove His claims by rising from
the dead as the one who has power over death. That is the divine context of the first public declaration of "world peace." It
is safe to say that the angelic host was not spouting off a well-
meaning but empty slogan to a handful of people and animals.
It is safe to say that the angelic multitude knew what they
were singing about. They sang that the true hope of peace on
earth was more than an idea. Peace was an idea now embodied
in a newborn baby, lying in a lowly feeding trough.

Cliché Jesus or Meaningful Jesus?

It is interesting that in contemporary secular circles and even
in nominally Christian circles of our day there is a tendency

to make Jesus Himself into a cliché. We often hear such sentiments as "Jesus would not judge; He would just love," or, "Jesus
preached peace" and would not support confrontation. How often we are given a depiction of an austere Jesus, who speaks
only softly and in even tones. He would never raise His voice.
He is gentle. He has a perpetual, ethereal look on His face. He
would never say a harsh word to anyone. He walks around in
slow, measured paces with His gaze always skyward. He speaks
with a mild-mannered tone that is almost asking to be ignored.
He does not believe in objective moral values, and He does not
make exclusive claims. In secular and contemporary depictions,
Jesus is the quintessential "nice guy." Simply put, popular culture tries to render Jesus as nonthreatening and ineffectual.

This is Cliché Jesus. This is the Jesus that liberals and rela-
tivists claim allegiance to. Cliché Jesus is the one whom bumper stickers refer to in saying, "Who Would Jesus Bomb?" in an
attempt to characterize as being hypocritical those who sometimes choose the necessary evil of war. Cliché Jesus is so vacuous a person that He *should* be ignored. Cliché Jesus' ideals and
sentiments are so lofty and esoteric that we cannot relate to
Him, we cannot listen to Him, and, therefore, we cannot actually follow Him. I venture to say that if Cliché Jesus were asked,
"What is the one most important thing our society needs?" He
would respond in character and spit out the ultimate cliché,
"World peace." He would not offer any real solutions, and He
would not challenge us to make any decisions to achieve them.

But as we shall soon see, Cliché Jesus is really only imagi-
nary. He is not the Jesus who actually walked the hills of Galilee
and spoke to and moved the masses throughout Judea.

Meaningful Jesus is the real Jesus of history. It is true that
Meaningful Jesus was austere and sometimes lofty. It is true
that He was sometimes soft-spoken. It is true that He was forgiving. But it is equally true that He was practical. Meaningful
Jesus engaged people on a real level, dealing with their present-
day problems. But He also pointed them to the blessings and
hope of a life beyond their circumstances. Meaningful Jesus

was confrontational and opinionated. He did not withhold His views or refrain from judgment because someone might be offended or have his or her feelings hurt. He repeatedly saw past the niceties of diplomacy and exposed the issues of the day for what they were, so that they could be dealt with. Meaningful Jesus was a welcome guest at a private dinner, yet He was a powerful public speaker. He was a dialoguer and a debater. Meaningful Jesus was compassionate, yet judgmental. When He saved the adulterous woman from those who were going to stone her for her sin, He said that He would not condemn her, but He made it clear that she must give up her life of sin. "Neither do I condemn you," He said to her, but also, "Go and sin no more" (John 8:11).

Cliché Jesus could not have encountered the Samaritan woman at Jacob's well in the profound way that Meaningful Jesus did. Cliché Jesus would not have exposed her prejudices. He would have glossed over them and patronizingly told her to "hang in there." Only Meaningful Jesus, the actual Jesus of history, could have liberated her as He did.

There is one thing that Cliché Jesus and Meaningful Jesus have in common. Were they both asked the question, "What is the one thing society needs?" they both would answer, "World peace." But there end the similarities. Cliché Jesus and Meaningful Jesus would define that term in very different ways. Cliché Jesus would define peace according to the common usage, as a lack of conflict. Meaningful Jesus had a more profound notion about the one thing society needs. On the first Christmas two thousand years ago—on that night, in that field, and to those shepherds—the Angel of the Lord and the heavenly host announced the arrival of the Son of God who would bring meaning to the sentiment, "peace on earth."

What Is Peace?

What is that "peace on earth" that was announced so many centuries ago? It certainly does not seem to mean divine intervention that would make us love and forgive one another. The past two thousand years since the angelic announcement have been marked and marred by violence and strife. Indeed, the most recent decades have been the bloodiest in history as we have devised newer and more wide-ranging means of destroying each other. Given all this, it seems impossible to imagine that the angel of the Lord really intended to announce that with Jesus' birth and the Messiah's coming conflict would end and suffering would cease. Still, the usage of the word *peace* gives us the true intent of the announcement and the meaning behind centuries of prophecy regarding the advent of peace on earth and what it really is.

As I mentioned above, Jesus has a fundamentally different idea about peace than what we typically think of. During his earthly ministry, Jesus made a statement that contradicts today's caricature of Him as a gentle pacifist whose sole mission in life was to teach us to stop fighting. Jesus, being the consummate realist that He is, says to us in Matthew 10:34–36:

> Don't assume that I came to bring peace on the earth. I did not come to bring peace, but a sword. For I came to turn a man against his father, a daughter against her mother, a daughter-in-law against her mother-in-law; and a man's enemies will be the members of his household. (HCSB)

This statement certainly shatters the images we have of Jesus as the tender mystic who only wanted to get us to group hug. Indeed, this statement is so strong that it might seem to be a direct contradiction to the angel's announcement to the shepherds at Jesus' birth.

But it is not. In announcing peace on earth to the shepherds that night, the angelic host made two proclamations in one statement. They announced both the incarnation of the embodiment of peace and a future hope for humanity, a blessing as it were. The angels announced that with the coming of the

Messiah, the age of true peace would eventually have its fulfillment. This was, in a sense, the announcement of the beginning of the end. That end is not a fearful, ominous one though. Rather, the angel announced the beginning of the end of this age of enmity between God and humanity and the coming of the age of reconciliation.

So what is Jesus saying in Matthew 10:34? The context of Jesus' statement gives us the full picture of what He is saying. In the verses preceding the quote, Jesus explains that those who follow Him will be persecuted and challenged to abandon their faith in Him. He predicted that there would be great opposition to those who found the truth in Jesus and that they would be tempted by intense and diverse pressures to deny Him (Matt. 10:16–25). Knowing the human heart and understanding the dynamics of family relationships, Jesus points out that the strongest of pressures are not physical, nor do they come from governmental authorities. Rather, the strongest pressure comes from our most intimate relationships. Those closest to a Christian sometimes are those who are most ardently at odds with him or her. In Matthew 10:34, Jesus says that human beings are divisive by nature and that we will divide over nothing more readily than the very person and work of Jesus Christ.

Has that not been the case? The ancient records tell us that the people in Judea were divided over Jesus. While the masses flocked to Him, the religious leaders envied and hated Him. Eventually, the Romans distrusted Him, and together they all wanted Him crucified. Later, the Romans persecuted Christians *en masse*, throwing them and their children to the lions, making them a spectacle because they would not renounce Christ as King and the incarnate God in favor of Caesar.

The human-made division over Jesus did not end even after Christianity had transformed the heart of the Roman Empire. Today, we can engage in a healthy, spirited discussion about religion, but at the mention of Jesus' name by one who believes in Meaningful Jesus, the conversation gets much louder or quickly grows silent. One can speak of diverse religious heritages in school or the public square, but we cannot discuss Jesus' nature and self-understanding in a classroom or display a nativity scene in a public place without worrying about being derided or even prosecuted. No person in history divides more deeply and sparks more controversy than Jesus. But as Jesus points out, the sharpest felt and most difficult opposition to overcome comes not from the public square, but from our closest relationships.

We freely choose to accept or reject Jesus. Those within the same family who are on the opposite ends of that decision will usually be at odds. Indeed, that was the case in Jesus' own family. Jesus' half-brother James was critical of Jesus and felt that He was deluded into thinking Himself to be God's Messiah (Mark 3:21, 31; John 7:5).[2] Two thousand years ago, Jesus experienced the very division He was speaking of and predicted that the division over His mission would persist throughout the ages. And He has been proved right.

So today's skeptic might say that from what he sees, religion offers us nothing when it comes to achieving world peace. In fact, he might say that religion has offered us quite the opposite, for where religious convictions are the most strongly held, there, too, will be the fiercest conflicts. It is a fair observation. However, the skeptic often forgets that in just the past century, the antireligious regimes of Hitler, Pol Pot, Stalin, Mao Tze Tung, and a host of others have caused the deaths of millions more than those caused by the religiously induced killing of the nineteen previous centuries combined. Dylan Kliebold and Eric Harris stomped trench-coated and jackbooted through the halls of Columbine High School in Colorado, not with a cross in hand, but with nihilism in mind. The point is this: Whether it is Christianity, atheism, or any other worldview, we should not judge the merits of that worldview by its abuse. Each worldview must be judged on the merits of its particular teachings and ideas.

Still the skeptic might protest, "Conflict is everywhere,

and it has been everywhere for the twenty centuries since those angels supposedly wished us all peace. How, then, can Christianity claim to have the cure for our ills?" It is a powerful question and one of the utmost importance. But it is not only for Christianity to address. Every worldview that claims to truly explain the human condition and provide a meaningful hope for changing that condition must answer such a question. But the Christian worldview provides an answer like no other worldview. And the answer lies in understanding the true nature of the peace that the heavenly host proclaimed. Were the angels speaking of peace as the absence of conflict and the ceasing of wars? Let us examine Jesus' words, for they give us an answer to that question.

Not as the World Gives

Jesus' idea of meaningful peace is not as simple as the absence of conflict. Of course, like every other word, *peace* has various definitions, and the context in which a word is found determines the appropriate definition. In Matthew 10:34, Jesus said that He did not come to bring peace in the worldly sense of the term. Jesus was a realist and knew that humans, having both a free will and a sinful nature, would immediately divide when faced with the claim that He is the Savior of the world. The worldly idea of peace is the absence of conflict, a lack of hostility among people. Jesus' intention was not to bring such superficial peace. In fact, he predicted that just the opposite would happen. As we will see, Jesus brought peace, but it is a much more meaningful and useful kind of peace.

We begin to understand what Jesus means by peace when we see how He used the term during the last hours before His death. In John 14 we find Jesus in intimate conversation with His disciples. On the night before He was to face the unspeakable violence of Roman scourging and crucifixion, He offered the disciples peace.

Peace I leave with you. *My peace* I give to you. I do not give to you as the world gives. Your heart must not be troubled or fearful. (John 14:27 HCSB, emphasis added)

Think of it. Jesus knew He was facing excruciating torture the next day and eventually the most agonizing death the world's mightiest power could devise to inflict. Yet He had peace. In fact, Jesus had such a profound peace that He offered it to His disciples, who were not facing imminent death. If true peace is the absence of conflict, then Jesus should have been the last person in that group to feel any sense of peace. The absence of conflict is the secular world's definition of peace, and it is a superficial definition. That is not the way Jesus defines peace.

The Hebrew word for peace is *shalom*, the Arabic word is *salaam*, and the Aramaic word is similar to both (Jesus spoke both Hebrew and Aramaic). The words *shalom* and *salaam* do not connote merely an absence of conflict. They share a more fundamental meaning and definition. Both words connote a state of being whole, being completed, at rest, and reconciled.[3] Both Hebrew and Arabic are Semitic languages, so it is not surprising that *shalom* and *salaam* would sound alike and share a common definition. What is surprising, however, is that the non-Semitic, Greek word for peace, *eirene*, shares the same definition with *shalom* and *salaam*. It does not mean simply a lack of conflict, but also a state of being "set at one" and having reconciliation in relationships.[4] Luke used *eirene* to communicate the heavenly host's announcement of Jesus' birth, and the apostle John used *eirene* to communicate the peace that Jesus offered to His disciples. The angelic host was announcing the advent of the one through whom reconciliation would be achieved. And Jesus offered His disciples the kind of peace that is manifest in being "set at one" again with God.

Not only does the secular view of peace fail to provide such depth of meaning, but it also shows its inadequacy by failing even to correspond with our everyday experiences. I recently heard the story of two sisters who are at such odds that they have not spoken to one another in fourteen years. There is no open conflict in that relationship, but it certainly is not peaceful. During the Cold War, the United States and the Soviet Union threatened each other and the entire world with annihilation. There was no violence between the nations, but one would be hard-pressed to call their relations peaceful. Real peace does not depend solely on the absence of violence. In fact, real peace does not depend solely on the existence or nonexistence of conflict. The popular definition of peace fails to capture this truth. It requires a lack of conflict, so it is only partially correct, which makes it completely wrong.

Perceiving this limited view of peace, Jesus offers peace "not as the world gives" (John 14:27). He offers the kind of peace that only the Son of God can give. The secular worldview defines peace in its own way, and most religious systems similarly define it as the absence of conflict or suffering. Indeed, Eastern religions try to attain "inner peace" by denying the existence of suffering or conflict. But the peace that Jesus gives is the only peace that does not run from conflict. Rather, the beauty of the peace Christ offers blossoms even in the presence of conflict.

This is why I believe Jesus offered not just peace but *His* peace to the disciples that night when violence loomed around the corner. Notice His careful wording in John 14:27. He said, "*My* peace I give to you." No doubt, Jesus wanted His disciples to remember in the difficult years to come that on the eve of His terrible suffering, He had peace, and He offered it to them. This was important because although the disciples did not know it that night, they would face violence and even death for following Jesus.

Stephen, one of the earliest followers of Jesus, would face martyrdom in just weeks with the peace only Jesus could give. Acts 7 recounts how Stephen was stoned to death for preaching the gospel of Jesus. The accounts of stoning do not provide us with the gruesome details. It was a brutal way to be killed.

Often, the condemned would be thrown into a deep pit and a large rock would be hurled onto the chest, crushing the ribs. Then the crowd would hurl stones at the condemned, striking the head, the body, the limbs, and the genitals with great force and blinding pain. Death was seldom quick. Yet remarkably, Luke tells us in Acts 7 that as Stephen was in the final moments of that very agony, he had the peace of mind and peace of spirit to utter as his final words, "Lord, do not charge them with this sin!" (Acts 7:60 HCSB). Stephen's martyrdom illustrates for us that the depth of the peace Jesus offers to His disciples does not depend on the absence of conflict, but stems from a sense of being reconciled to God *in the very midst of conflict.* That peace is of a different quality than the peace offered by the world. The world seeks peace in the form of an end to conflict, but it misses the fact that we cannot have an end to conflict with one another until we have a peace within that comes from being reconciled ourselves to God. The end of conflict begins with the kind of peace that seeks the welfare of the very people bent on killing us. Stephen was imparted that kind of peace as he died preaching Christ's resurrection as the hope for those who gnashed their teeth at him.

The New Testament and history tell us that Jesus' disciples and other early followers also met death or suffered because they preached the same message to Jews and non-Jews alike. Peter and Paul were imprisoned, beaten, and put to death because they claimed that Jesus had risen from the dead in confirmation of His divine claims. Others met with similar persecution, and John was exiled to the island of Patmos, where he wrote the book of Revelation.[5]

We briefly touched on the enmity that existed within Jesus' own household. But Jesus' half-brother James's inner conflict with Jesus gave way to reconciliation because James came to realize that Jesus' claim to provide true peace was validated. Jesus died an ignominious death on a cross, or was "hanged on a tree," as it were. To the Jew, one who "is hanged is accursed" (Deut. 21:23 KJV). But Jesus' death did not vindicate James's derision. Instead, it transformed James because he saw that Jesus did not stay dead. Indeed, history tells us that James became the leader of the Jerusalem church.[6] Eventually, James went to his death, not for an ideal or a principal, but for the fact that with his own eyes he beheld Jesus risen from the dead in confirmation of His claims to be divine and the Messiah.[7] If James had not really seen the risen Jesus after the crucifixion, he would have known the claim to be false. Yet he lived according to that claim and died for that claim. It is, frankly, incredible to think that James would willingly die for a fact he knew to be false. The more likely explanation is that James had truly seen his half-brother Jesus risen from the dead. It was that fact that transformed James's enmity into loyalty. James was able to face up to persecution and violence—he was able to find peace during conflict—because he had received the *shalom*, the *salaam*, and the *eirene* that Jesus gave. That is what Jesus meant when He offered His own kind of peace. On the eve of His greatest suffering, and on the precipice of the apostolic age during which His closest followers would suffer violence, Jesus offered a peace that endured *despite* conflict.

In Luke 2, we see the beginning of true peace announced at Jesus' birth. In John 20, we see Jesus announcing the realization of that peace at His resurrection. In the evening on the day of Jesus' resurrection, some of His disciples were gathered in a house with the doors locked (John 20:19). The disciples were in hiding, fearing that they would be discovered as associates of the recently executed Jesus. In the midst of that locked house filled with the fearful, Jesus suddenly physically appeared to them. "Peace to you!" Jesus announced and showed them the scars in His hands from being crucified and the wound in His side from the Roman soldier's spear (John 20:20 HCSB). After showing them the proof that He had risen from the dead, He repeated His greeting to them, "Peace to you!" (John 20:21 HCSB).

Thomas, one of the original twelve disciples, was not with the other disciples when Jesus appeared to them in the locked home. Those who were there told Thomas of their encounter, but Thomas was skeptical. "If I don't see the mark of the nails in His hands, put my finger into the mark of the nails, and put my hand into His side, I will never believe!" he told them (John 20:25 HCSB). Eight days later, Thomas was gathered with some disciples, again in a locked room. Again, Jesus came to them physically and announced, "Peace to you!" Jesus stood face-to-face with the skeptical Thomas. He showed Thomas the nail scars and the wound in His side. Flooded with peace, Thomas finally did believe and jubilantly called Him "My Lord and My God" (John 20:28 HCSB).

Serious doubt is a state of conflict. It is a state of conflict between what one side of your mind tells you and what the evidence tells you. Serious doubt in certain contexts causes fear and a lack of true peace. The disciples had been in fear and spiritual disquiet because the authorities had executed their leader, Jesus. They gathered secretly, fearing that they would be discovered to be followers of Jesus. Jesus came to them, passing through the locked doors, which had come to embody their state of fear, and three times said to them, "Peace to you." When Jews greet each other, they say, "Shalom alaichem." When Arabs greet one another, they say, "As-salaamu alaikum," a similar sounding phrase. Both phrases mean, "Peace to you." Jesus undoubtedly said this phrase many times to His disciples and others He greeted. But these instances in John 20 are the only recordings of His use of the greeting. In fact, Jesus used the greeting conspicuously in one instance even after He had first greeted the disciples. In the initial postresurrection encounter with His disciples, He gave them the greeting when He first came into the locked room (John 20:19). He repeated the greeting after He had shown them the proof that He was physically risen from the dead (John 20:21). Perhaps John was inspired to record these particular instances of Jesus saying "Peace to you" because they are especially poignant. In saying, "Peace to you" the second time, Jesus was not being redundant. Rather, He was telling the disciples that their inner conflicts, their fears, and their disquiets are resolved by the reality of Christ's resurrection from the dead.

The disciples once hid in locked rooms out of fear of the authorities who had slain Jesus. After seeing the risen Jesus, they preached the significance of Jesus' death and resurrection to those same authorities. Tradition tells us that the once fearful and doubting Thomas took the certainty of that peace with him to India. There, through the preaching of the gospel, he was instrumental in transforming Hindus from pantheistic and polytheistic slaves to karma, into those who found freedom and peace in their newfound bondage to Christ. Ultimately, Thomas was martyred for his faith while serving the Lord in India, and to this day a monument stands in his honor in Chennai, India.[8] Jesus gave the disciples peace and allayed their fears. Before His death, Jesus promised to give them peace "not as the world gives" (John 14:27). Having risen from the dead, Jesus delivered on that promise.

The Eternality of True Peace

Jesus understood what kind of peace the world gives. He understood that such peace is only fleeting. Have we not seen age-old enemies lay down their arms only to take them up again? Have we not witnessed an aggressor nation cease its persecutions of one people only to redirect its hostilities elsewhere? Have we not seen the oppressed overthrow their rulers only to become the oppressors themselves? Of course, there is value in striving for the end of aggression and hostility. But is there any *lasting* value in seeking to end one episode of hostility without trying to impart the source of true peace and the need for the most fundamental kind of reconciliation, reconciliation between God and sinners?

The world seeks peace *only* through treaties and accords. Such treaties and accords may temporarily stop the violence in one part of the world, but the underlying hostility remains. Seeking peace in this way is only treating the symptoms rather than the disease of conflict. Jesus tells us that there is no permanent, lasting value to such peace without divine reconciliation. When we obtain the material or worldly solution without the spiritual, we are only temporarily satisfied and soon need something more. Knowing this, Jesus offers us a permanent, spiritual peace. He tells us that when we drink of that which He offers, we will never thirst again, but will have so much that it wells up within us and can be imparted to others (John 4:13–14).

The angelic host in Luke 2 announced the fulfillment of a prophecy made centuries before about the birth of one who would impart true peace. The prophet Isaiah was given the divine prophecy of the birth of a child and the giving of a son who would take upon Himself the task of bringing about true peace between God and humanity.

> For a child will be born for us, a son will be given to us, and the government will be on His shoulders. He will be named Wonderful Counselor, Mighty God, Eternal Father, Prince of Peace. (Isa. 9:6 HCSB)

As Ravi Zacharias points out, we can note two important things in this prophecy. First, the "child" is "born," but the "son" is "given." We see in this passage the details of the incarnation of Christ. In his human nature, He was born into this world as a child. But Jesus' divine nature knows no beginning. That divine nature, which is God the Son in the triune Godhead, could not be born as it were. Rather, the divine Son could only be *given*. Incarnate in the Child who was born is the transcendent Son who was given.[9] In both His human nature and divine nature, Jesus was a gift to the world, the one who was and is the Prince of Peace.

That peace of which He is the Prince is true *shalom*. It is true *salaam*. It is true *eirene*. Peace as Jesus defines it and as the heavenly host announced it at His birth, however, is fundamentally different from the world's peace because it is not just horizontal; it is both horizontal and vertical. Jesus is God incarnate, the eternal Word made flesh, the Son of God, very God of very God. He did not just claim this about Himself and then die in obscurity. He died for the claim and rose from the dead to validate His claim. Jesus is one of the persons of the triune Godhead. His personhood as the Son is distinct from that of God the Father and God the Holy Spirit. Yet His nature is one and the same with theirs. As such, He is a being existing in eternal relationship, a being "at rest." Thus, there is a horizontal quality to Jesus' divine relationships. But Jesus also has a human nature, which must be, and is, "set at one" with the divine. Jesus, as the God-man, as the only one to have both divine and human natures, has both the vertical peace with God and the horizontal peace with humanity. If true *shalom, salaam,* or *eirene* is the peace that comes from being "set at one again," then Jesus is the very embodiment of that peace in the sharing of human nature with divine nature in the one person, Jesus Christ. Only one who is both fully God and fully man could provide the reconciliation between God and man that is needed as the fundamental ingredient of peace on earth.

In Jesus, true peace, the true *shalom, salaam,* or *eirene,* is complete. The peace that is characteristic of Jesus' existence is an analogy for the peace He offers to us. He offers us the vertical reconciliation with God by providing propitiation for our sins. He offers us peace with one another, for when we realize the vertical reconciliation, we see other men and women as those who do not need to be killed but need to be offered that same peace that is freely given to us. That peace is a rest and quietness with those with whom we are equal, and, more importantly, with the one who has no equal.

Jesus had peace on that night before He was tortured because He had confidence in the reconciling power of God. The poetry of the peace offered by Jesus is that each one of us can know that peace that comes from spiritual reconciliation with God and with one another only *because* Jesus underwent unspeakable violence. The disciples knew that peace after having witnessed

Jesus' resurrection, and thus they faced their own violent deaths with tremendous peace. This reconciliation that brings about peace was achieved only through the crucifixion—one of the most violent acts ever inflicted on an innocent person. As we have seen, Jesus' peace is profound because it is peace that exists despite conflict and that finds its full expression during conflict. As we will see next, it is a peace that we can know only because Jesus experienced a particular conflict in our place.

Chapter 5

THE CRUX OF THE MATTER

Resolving Sorrow, Justice, and Love at the Cross

Get behind me, Satan!" Jesus shouted to Peter, one of his closest and most trusted disciples (Matt. 16:23). It was a shocking rebuke and must have hurt Peter deeply. But it was necessary. Jesus' rebuke came in a somewhat strange context. Jesus was with his disciples near Caesarea Philippi when he asked them a very important question: "Who do you say that I am?" (Matt. 16:15). The disciples had been with Jesus for over a year at this point, yet it was still important for Jesus to make sure they understood who He was and the true purpose for His coming to earth.

When Jesus asked the question, the hot-blooded Peter immediately spoke up, saying, "You are the Messiah, the Son of the living God" (Matt. 16:16 HCSB). It was the truth, and it was a profound truth about Jesus' identity.

In response, Jesus told Peter in front of the other disciples, "Blessed are you . . . because flesh and blood did not reveal this to you, but My Father in heaven" (Matt. 16:17 HCSB).

On the heels of that exchange, Jesus and Peter's interaction took a sudden and unexpected turn. We read that after Peter's revelation about Christ's identity, Jesus began to explain to His disciples that He "must" go to Jerusalem, suffer at the hands of the elders, chief priests, and the scribes, be killed, and be raised on that third day (Matt. 16:21). These were words Peter did not want to hear. As we discussed in chapter 2, Peter had a specific idea of the Messiah's role in stamping out corruption in the religious hierarchy and ridding Israel of Roman rule. With this new information, Jesus was challenging all of Peter's assumptions and perhaps even the very reason Peter had chosen to follow Jesus in the first place. With characteristic emotionality, Peter took Jesus aside and even rebuked Him for saying such things, "God forbid it, Lord! This shall never happen to You," he told Jesus (Matt. 16:22 NASB).

In response to Peter's rebuke, Jesus came back with an even stronger rebuke. "Get behind me, Satan!" Jesus exclaimed. "You are a stumbling block to Me; for you are not setting your mind on God's interests, but man's" (Matt. 16:23 NASB).

Peter's struggle with Jesus' revelation of His imminent suffering and death arose because of Peter's preconceived notions about the Messiah's role in bringing peace and an end to conflict. Peter and the disciples lived in a country of conflict. The religious leaders were corrupt, and the government was run by a pagan foreign power that had seized control by force. Around 4 B.C., 2,000 Jews attempted a rebellion, only to be publicly crucified by the Roman general Varus as a shameful display of what would befall those who opposed Rome.[1] Living in that conflict-ridden context, Peter had lived with feelings of sorrow, injustice, and a lack of love his entire life. In Jesus, he had seen the possibility of ending that sorrow, righting the injustice, and proving God's love through political and military conquest. He had envisioned the resolution of these issues in Jesus, but not in the way in which God had planned that resolution.

In fact, we read that after rebuking Peter, Jesus said to all the disciples, "If anyone wants to come with Me, he must deny himself, take up his cross, and follow Me" (Matt. 16:24 HCSB). This verse has a universal application to our lives today, but we should never forget its specific context. Jesus said this *to His disciples* on the heels of Peter's statement of his aspirations for revolt. May I suggest that Jesus was telling the disciples in general, and Peter in particular, that they needed to put away their human-driven notions of what it means to resolve the issues of sorrow, justice, and love. Peter envisioned a peace that would come when sorrow, justice, and love would be resolved in Jerusalem and at the temple, where the Romans and the religiously corrupt would be vanquished. Jesus had something far different in mind. Sorrow, justice, and love would find their resolution on a Roman cross on a desolate hill outside Jerusalem's gates, at a place ominously called Golgotha—"The Place of the Skull."

It is hardly an inviting name for a place. Even the sound of the name Golgotha is harsh and guttural. It conjures up grim images of death and decay. The use to which that small plot of land was put—the punishment of criminals—made the place even more foreboding. I often imagine that those who passed by that place in the first century took the long way around it, careful not to tread on its soil out of superstitious fear. They would not spend too much time close to that place and would not let their gaze linger on it. If the people found themselves staring at that spot, it was likely out of morbid fascination, much like tourists today who visit Alcatraz.

In previous chapters, we have seen that true peace is that quality that not only endures conflict but also blossoms from conflict. At Golgotha, the quintessential conflict took place, and there we find all three elements of conflict expressed and addressed. That historical reality is at the very heart of the gospel of peace that Jesus and His disciples preached. It has been rightly said that there is no Christianity without the cross. A cross-less gospel is no gospel at all. Jesus did not leave it to us to determine whether it was simply His teaching of good moral values that should be followed or the cross that we should embrace. While His wisdom and guidance are important facets of His mission, they are ancillary to the primary reason that God determined to intersect human history in the incarnation of Jesus. He tells us directly that the crucifixion, Jesus' death on the cross as the eternal payment for sin, was the very reason He came to this world (John 12:27–33). I have maintained that the gospel is the only means by which the issues of sorrow, justice, and love arising from conflict can be resolved. If the cross is the very center of the gospel, then it is from the cross that resolution comes.

Sorrow at the Place of the Skull

The cry of sorrow rises up from many voices and from many contexts. Natural disasters, tragic accidents, sickness, and war provide the causes for sorrow. The fundamental nature of sorrow, however, is that it emanates from an intense feeling of loss. We feel sorrow when we lose possessions, when we lose loved ones, when we lose relationships, and when we see we are about to lose our own life. I have often watched the television reports on the Middle East conflict or sat down with someone close to me who has lost something or someone because of that conflict. I have seen the bottomless depths to their gazes, and I have heard the strangled anguish in their voices. Yet I have not become accustomed to it, and I pray that I never will. The gazes and voices all display a commonality: profound loss. In the all-too-frequent suicide bombings and air strikes, the sorrowful lose their homes, their children, their spouses, and their very lives.

Where do we turn to find answers to the questions that spring from such loss? To whom can we turn to find one who identifies with the pangs we feel in such grief? Is there anyone among the founders of the various worldviews and religions who can tell us that they know what we have gone through and can offer us hope that what has been lost can be restored? Which worldview offers us an ultimate authority who has a kinship with us in our sorrow?

Jesus of Nazareth walked this earth, having both divine

and human natures. That reality is not the same as the Eastern or New Age mysticism, where the divine is "within" humanity, but undiscovered. Jesus' human nature is truly human, which is to say that it is not at all divine. His divine nature is utterly divine, in that it is not at all human. Yet within the person of Jesus, both natures coexist without commingling. Jesus is not half-man and half-God. He is fully man and fully God. He is at once the man Christ Jesus and Jesus, the Son of God.

This is important to understand because in His divinity, the Son of God has eternal, unbroken communion with the other persons in the Godhead, God the Father and God the Holy Spirit. In the Trinity, God exists in a state of eternal relationship within Himself. In His humanity, Jesus has intimate communion with God. In the person of Christ, there is a bond and relationship between God and humanity that is so intense in its intimacy that it is indescribable. No natural relationship that we can look to in our worldly experience can compare with Jesus' supernatural relationships. Thus, no break or loss in natural relationships can compare with the intensity of sorrow that would come from any break in the relationship between Jesus' human nature and the divine.

The pain of a severed connection is directly proportional to the strength of the connection. A child's tooth, hanging by only a thread of nerve painlessly falls out, but even the thought of a deeply rooted molar wrenched from its socket pains the imagination. In the conflict at Golgotha, the unfathomably strong relationship between Jesus' humanity and God was ruptured. The human mind cannot even apprehend the resultant agony and sorrow. In the Garden of Gethsemane on the night He was betrayed, Jesus was rocked by intense sorrow as the impending agony grew near. He went to seek fellowship with God and told His disciples, "My soul is swallowed up in sorrow—to the point of death" (Matt. 26:38, Mark. 14:34 HCSB). We read further that in His emotional anguish, Jesus cried out to God, "*Abba*, Father! All things are possible for You. Take this cup away from Me. Nevertheless, not what I will, but what You will" (Mark. 14:36 HCSB).

But why? What was so remarkable about the anguish of sorrow that Jesus was feeling that caused Him to cry out to God, His Father, in this way? It is an especially important question because some have used these passages to argue that Jesus did not want to go through the crucifixion, and thus perhaps God rescued Him from it.[2] It is especially important also because it highlights the true depth of what Jesus was willing to do for the sake of humanity's salvation.

There can be no doubt that Jesus willingly accepted His mission to sacrifice Himself on the cross. Although He asked if God the Father could take the "cup" away from Him, He stood firm in His conviction to carry out God's will, which was that He offer Himself up as the sacrifice for the sins of the world (Matt. 26:39, 42; Mark. 14:36). In fact, Jesus said in His second prayer, "My Father, if this cannot pass unless I drink it, Your will be done" (Matt. 26:42 HCSB). Jesus was not saying that He was not willing to undergo the crucifixion. Rather, He was expressing His desire that a particular kind of anguish would pass from Him as He fulfilled the very purpose for which He came to earth. John Stott puts it this way:

> What is this cup? Is it physical suffering from which he shrinks, the torture of the scourge and the cross, together perhaps with the mental anguish of betrayal, denial and desertion by his friends, and the mockery and abuse of his enemies? Nothing could ever make me believe that the cup Jesus dreaded was any of these things (grievous as they were) or all of them together. His physical and moral courage throughout his public ministry had been indomitable. To me it is ludicrous to suppose that he was now afraid of pain, insult and death.[3]

Stott goes on to convincingly argue that Jesus could not have been shrinking from the physical torture and mental anguish because Jesus had long predicted that that day would come. He had even insisted that His suffering must occur when His own disciples tried to talk Him out of it. Indeed, Jesus had taught His disciples to rejoice in suffering for the sake of the truth. So, it would seem unfathomable that Jesus would now shirk the physical suffering set before Him.[4]

As Stott points out, and as we do well to remember, the anguish that Jesus hoped would pass was not the physical torture He would soon endure. Rather, Jesus dreaded a loss of much more than just His blood. As Stott correctly explains,

> The cup from which he shrank was something different. It symbolized neither the physical pain of being flogged and crucified, nor the mental distress of being despised and rejected even by his own people, but rather the spiritual agony of bearing the sins of the world—in other words, of enduring the divine judgment that those sins deserved. That this is the correct understanding is strongly confirmed by the Old Testament usage, for in both the Wisdom literature and the Prophets the Lord's "cup" was a regular symbol of his wrath.[5]

What was it about experiencing God's wrathful judgment for the sins of the world on the cross that made Jesus dread it so? Jesus' words provide us with a glimpse of the profundity of the loss that made Him so sorrowful.

In the Garden of Gethsemane, Jesus cried out to God as "*Abba*, Father" (Mark 14:36). The Aramaic word *abba* is a term of endearment, used by a child to address his father. The closest English translation would be something similar to "Daddy."[6] When we hear a child call his father "Daddy," we hear in that term both respect and endearment. That word conveys the kind of closeness of relationship that dry addresses such as "Father" cannot convey. Thus, in His moment of intense emotion, while on the brink of terrible suffering, Jesus referred to God as "Daddy." This reflects how sharply focused Jesus was on the closeness of His relationship with God. The reason for such focus was that He knew that for the true work of the cross to be accomplished—for sin to be punished and paid for there—the relationship between Jesus in His humanity and God the Father would have to be ruptured in order for the fullness of God's wrath to be poured out on Jesus.

It was not that the divine relationship between God the Son and God the Father would be ruptured. That would be an impossible division within the Godhead. It was not that the divine nature and the human nature shared by Jesus would be severed, because that would be an impossible separation within the person of Christ. Rather, the relationship between Jesus in His humanity and God in His holy divinity would have to be ruptured because Jesus, who knew no sin, would take on the sins of the entire world. We will address the facet of justice in Jesus' sacrifice in the coming pages. Suffice it to say for now, however, that sin is impure by definition and is rebellion against God. God is pure and therefore cannot abide sin. Thus, as Jesus took on the world's sins, a rupture between Jesus in His humanity and God was necessary. Though the rupture would be temporally limited, it was qualitatively unfathomable. Seeing the magnitude of the pain from this unimaginable loss of intimacy, Jesus cried out to "Daddy," as it were. The stress of His sorrow was so intense, in fact, that Luke the physician tells us that Jesus underwent something akin to a condition called hematidrosis, in which intense stress causes the blood vessels on one's skin to burst and pour out droplets of blood.[7] Luke tells us that, "Being in anguish, [Jesus] prayed more fervently, and His sweat became like drops of blood falling to the ground" (Luke 22:44 HCSB).

At the cross, Jesus' sorrow from God's unmitigated wrath poured out on His humanity was so acute that Matthew (27:46) and Mark (15:34) record for us Jesus' cry, "My God, My God, why have You forsaken Me?" Skeptic and critic alike have asked, *If Jesus had a divine nature, wouldn't He know why He had been forsaken?* From the lips of some, these questions come as sincere inquiries. From the lips of others, these questions come only as challenges to the orthodox view of the incarnation. Yet there are many answers to these questions. Jesus did not ask this question to get information. He was not ignorant of what was happening to Him and why. But why did He ask the question?

Jesus' question was obviously a quotation of the first sentence of Psalm 22, which expresses the anguish of an innocent man undergoing unspeakable suffering. Jesus in His humanity, both in the human body and in the human spirit, actually had been forsaken by God. The most powerful relationship between Jesus' humanity and the divine was broken. As Jesus considered His momentous suffering—the culmination of thousands of years of Old Testament prophecy—His thoughts naturally turned to the Scriptures. With the exceptions of Job's cries and the Lamentations of Jeremiah, the Psalms are the most powerful biblical expressions of utter grief and sorrow. As Stott points out, Jesus expressed His sorrow by asking "why?" only because the psalm is worded that way.[8] There is a second reason Jesus quotes Psalm 22. Though Psalm 22 begins with a cry of abandonment and despair, it develops from despondency to victory. Jesus quoted Psalm 22 because He truly experienced abandonment, yet He clung to the knowledge that victory would eventually come.[9]

Justice at the Place of the Skull

It often has been asked, "Why the cross?" What makes it a necessary feature of the Christian faith? The answer is that God is perfectly holy and just. The answer is simple, but it certainly is not simplistic.

To a perfectly holy and just God, our sin, our willful disobedience and offenses against Him, must be punished or paid for. This is a basic and intuitive truth. As we proceed in the daily administration of human affairs, we depend on the consistency of this principle. The world operates and finds coherence by the application and enforcement of laws. When those laws are violated, the violation must be addressed, and the violator must be punished. Otherwise, the very nature of an ordered society, based on objective moral principles, breaks down into chaos. Chaos is the very antithesis of structured society. Society, by its nature, is nonchaotic. When crimes go unpunished and when debts go uncollected, however, a society changes into its own antithesis.

And so it is with the holy and just God described by the Bible. Holiness and justice are inseparable and immutable qualities of God's nature. Because they are immutable, they cannot be compromised in any way. If God's nature could be compromised, be it by circumstances or by an act of His own will, God would become inconsistent and mutable. This would mean that He is no longer eternally perfect and independent because His character would become context-dependent. All of His attributes must remain immutable and consistent. Otherwise, we would have no way to gauge whether we are following an objective truth because the very Creator of our existence ceases to be objectively knowable.

Since holiness and justice are two of God's attributes, they cannot be compromised. By definition they require satisfaction for wrongs committed or debts incurred, and sin is wrong committed and debt incurred against God. We can manifest sin in virtually unlimited misdeeds or failures to act. Our actions, our inactions, and our very thoughts can constitute these wrongs against God. Though sin can be manifested in almost unlimited ways, these manifestations are just expressions of sin's fundamental characteristic, which is rebellion against God. God, in His immutable holiness and justice must address this rebellion.

I have heard the common responses to this reasoning. If God is all-powerful, then why can't He just simply overlook sin or forgive it? If He is obligated in some way to punish sin, then He is bound by laws outside of Himself, and He is not omnipotent. At first blush, this seems to be a persuasive objection, but it is fatally flawed in that it posits an incoherent idea of what it means for God to be all-powerful. God's omnipotence should not be thought of simplistically in terms of raw power. To do so would lead to logical absurdities and contradictions. Rather, omnipotence must be thought of in the context of God's nature. It is His nature to be consistent, and it is His nature to be holy. Put simpler, He is consistently holy. To posit a God who could exercise such power contrary to His holy nature is to posit a God who can defy Himself and do what is not conceptually reasonable. In other words, by exercising raw power to act in a way that is contrary to His nature, God ceases to be Himself. If God could do evil, He would cease to be thoroughly good, which is essential to His nature. To talk of a God who could compromise His attributes is to talk about square circles or smelling the colors of numbers.[10]

Some argue that God could not and would not use the cross as a means for forgiving sins because if He were to allow His creation to subject Him to humiliation, this would somehow sully His divinity. But this view limits God even more. As Kenneth Cragg puts it, "Those who question the necessity of the Cross on the ground that forgiveness is effortless with God may be forbidding Him the will and power the cross can measure. That He may not stoop to *that* compassion is no less a prohibition by dogma than to believe he will not forgive without it."[11] In other words, to believe that God would not or could not willingly subject Himself to the cross does far worse than limit His majesty; it limits His compassion. It is His limitless majesty that causes us to be created; it is His limitless compassion that causes us to be redeemed.

Sin is very serious, and the cross illustrates its seriousness like nothing else. It was the eleventh-century theologian and philosopher Anselm, Archbishop of Canterbury, who explained this so well in his work *Cur Deus Homo?* where he wrote that if anybody imagines that God can simply forgive us as we forgive others, that person has "not yet considered what a heavy weight sin is."[12] Stott adds that when we say that God can simply forgive sin, we rob Him of His place as the holy Judge and put ourselves in His place. "For us to argue 'we forgive each other unconditionally, let God do the same to us' betrays not sophistication but shallowness, since it overlooks the elementary fact that we are not God."[13] The point is quite simple. We forgive others their wrongs against us because we are, in a very real sense, no better than they are and realize within ourselves that we are capable of the same kinds of acts (and probably have committed them). We extend forgiveness without justice for a number of reasons, but the most natural reason is that we hope that we will get the same kind of unjustified mercy in return when inevitably we fail others.

God does not share this same fear or insecurity. He does not live in a glass house that He should be afraid to throw stones. He cannot be called a hypocrite for judging and punishing someone for a shortcoming He may be guilty of Himself. His judgment of human sin is not a mere fit of pique. Instead, God is the only being who truly can be righteously indignant at our sin. We must be accommodating in judgment, and when human judgment is not accommodating, it devolves into vengeful anger. "Human anger," Stott says, "is usually arbitrary and uninhibited; divine anger is always principled and controlled."[14]

The view that God cannot simply forgive sins without some form of punishment also respects the concept of human moral agency and gives dignity to our choices. It has been said that God is not a cosmic rapist of the will. He grants us free will, mostly so that we can freely love Him, because only freely chosen love is a real love. To sincerely give full expression to that free will, God must impose consequences on both our good and evil choices. Thus, if God only rewarded the good but passed on the evil, He would act arbitrarily, compromising His just nature and robbing us of the freedom to choose in light of the consequences of our actions.

But there is more. If we hold to the idea that God is holy and just but is able and willing to simply forgive our sins, we believe a contradiction. By definition, perfect holiness and perfect justice cannot simply overlook sin. So to view God as one who simply forgives without payment or punishment is to diminish the perfection of His justice. As R. W. Dale puts it, "It is partly because sin does not provoke our own wrath that we do not believe that sin provokes the wrath of God."[15] Thus, to think of God in these terms is to make Him too much like us—to make God in our image, as it were. We make ourselves more comfortable with the level of our own merit by lowering the level of God's.

Thus, it does not limit God or detract from His omnipotence to say that He must punish sin. It is part of His holy and just nature to require payment for sin. God is ultimately just, and compromise in this area makes Him less than God. In fact, if God becomes any "less," then He actually ceases to be God. Just as an ordered society ceases its existence when it allows chaos to reign, so too God would cease to be God if He compromised His holiness or any of His attributes.

When we sin, we rebel against God; we have committed an eternal offense against the eternal God. But why should it be that an act committed in time and space should have consequences that persist eternally? The reason is because time actually has nothing to do with justice. The temporal brevity of a sinful act says nothing about the measurement of its depth. A murder can take but a second, while cheating on a test can drone on for hours. Yet the murder is immeasurably more heinous than cheating on a test. Sin is not just a temporary slip in character or a lapse in judgment. If we view sin so trivially, do we not make ourselves the arbiters of what is and is not deserving of punishment? Do we not make ourselves God? When we sin, we say to God that His will is not going to guide our morality and conduct. We say to Him that His will is subservient to ours. God is immeasurably holier and immeasurably greater than we are. But when we rebel, we consciously declare the opposite. We disrespect His eternality. Thus, sin is a conscious act done within the confines of time that makes a statement that echoes in eternity.

The gospel stands opposed to our efforts to debase God and exalt ourselves. The cross reveals the situation as it really is. The cross gives God His due and dignifies our choices. As Stott concludes,

> To dethrone God and enthrone ourselves not only dispenses with the cross; it also degrades both God and humans. A biblical view of God and ourselves, however—that is, of our sin and of God's wrath—honors both. It honors human beings by affirming them as responsible for their own actions. It honors God by affirming him as having moral character.[16]

In committing sin, we incur an eternal debt to God. No penalty we can endure in our temporal state can pay that debt. Only a punishment that transcends time and a payment that comes from the eternal can right our wrongs. We are not capable of taking such a punishment or making such a payment without the cost of our very souls and eternal separation from God. What hope, then, is there for us if God must satisfy His divine justice and punish sin?

The answer lies in the cross, which is the transcendent fulfillment of the foreshadowing rituals of atonement found in the Old Testament. Under the old covenant, atonement for the peoples' sins required an animal's death. In the Law of Moses, God had commanded an elaborate system of animal sacrifice that symbolized the punishment for sin. We also see atonement in the form of the scapegoat. The sins of the people were symbolically placed on the head of the scapegoat, and it was sent out into the wilderness to die, alone and separated from the community of God.[17] Through the Old Testament sacrificial system, we see the seriousness of sin and its costliness. Because the sacrifices were merely animals, however, the process would have to be repeated over and over again as the people continued to sin. The scapegoat was not eternal, and so its temporal blood and life would not satisfy judgment eternally. The ultimate hope had to lie in a future, eternal sacrifice that would satisfy the need for judgment on sin once and for all. Since sin is an eternal affront to God, only a payment with an eternal quality could provide atonement. As Cragg puts it, "The measure of the cost is the measure of the violation and everything, with God, is immeasurably greater."[18]

By definition, however, there is nothing and no one who is eternal but God. Thus, the eternal sacrifice would have to come from the divine. But how can this be accomplished? God in His nature cannot die. He is a necessary being, which is to say that there cannot be a state of affairs in which He does not exist. The beauty of God's incarnation in Jesus Christ provides the means for an eternally efficacious sacrifice. The relationship of the human and divine natures within the person of Jesus has an eternal, infinite quality. We find a sign of the eternality of Jesus' payment for sin in the fact that though Jesus' body was restored in His resurrection, there remained on His physical body the eternal scars of the crucifixion. His hand, His side, and His feet forever bear the simultaneous ugliness and splendor of His self-sacrifice. Though Jesus was physically raised, He was not merely physical. He was physical in an eternal sense. His post-resurrection physicality was not limited, as He was able to walk through locked doors (John 20:19, 26). Though He was glorified for eternity in this way, the evidence of the infinite price He paid would always be with Him. Often I have heard it said that Jesus' scars are a symbol of His eternal love, but seldom has it been pointed out that the scars are also the signs of eternal justice. Our sins against the eternal demand eternal penalties. The scars on Jesus' body demonstrate that He bears the eternal consequences forever. The import of God's incarnation in Jesus is that it provides for us both the corporeal and the eternal means to achieve the aims of justice.[19]

Love at the Place of the Skull

Love is characterized by giving. It is almost universally true that on birthdays, holidays, and anniversaries, we express our love to each other by giving gifts. In fact, in most cultures, the wedding ceremony is sealed when the bride and groom exchange gifts, usually rings. When we truly love someone, we give of our time, our treasure, and our strength. Amy Carmichael, who spent fifty-three years as a missionary in India without furlough, once wrote, "One can give without loving, but one cannot love without giving."[20] The point is clear. True love impels us to give to another.

While exchanging gifts on anniversaries and birthdays is all well and good, there is still a hint of "giving to get" in such exchanges. How often do we feel the guilt of having not given an expensive gift to a loved one after that person has just given us a present that we know far exceeds what we paid for his or her gift? That sense of guilt comes from our desire for reciprocity in gift giving. Thus, giving, in and of itself, is not the hallmark of pure love. Rather, there is a special kind of giving that demonstrates pure, selfless love.

The greatest expression of love is self-sacrifice. When we think of God, we are thinking of a being who possesses infinitely positive attributes and who expresses them in the ultimate ways. We can think of no being with higher moral attributes or higher expressions of those moral attributes than God. If love is one of those attributes, as the Bible says it is when it states that "God is love," then no other being could express that attribute in a form that is higher or more admirable.[21]

Yet we see human beings providing the ultimate expression of love through self-sacrifice for the benefit of others. Indeed, people even give their very lives for the welfare of others. A parent gives to an infant when the child is practically nothing but a burden. There is, from a purely economical view, very little reciprocity of relationship. Yet a parent will pour everything he or she has into a child, unconditionally. As I grew up, my parents and my Middle Eastern heritage, in which family is of the utmost importance, constantly reminded me of this fact.[22] Just a few short years ago, those lectures and platitudes suddenly became very real as my world changed with the birth of my first child. In a moment of time, unconditional love changed from an abstract idea into a compelling force that drives me to pour myself into a young life no matter what the personal sacrifice will be. What father or mother reading these words would not gladly give their very life to save the life of their child? Those who believe that God could not or would not deign to save us through the Cross rob Him of the ultimate expression of love. Would we have it that the very God who created us be incapable of or even unwilling to express love in this ultimate way? Are we capable of being more loving than He?

The very thought seems strange if such a being as God exists. The solution must be that God is fully capable of self-sacrifice in some sense. Only the Christian faith offers this solution in the incarnation of Jesus and His work on the cross. When we give our own lives for those we love, we give up the physical part of existence. Our souls continue on, but our bodies do not. In an analogous fashion, God also gives something up. This brings the realities of the Trinity, God existing in one essence in three distinct persons, and the incarnation, the person of Jesus possessing two distinct natures, into full view. God the Son must willingly *choose* to share the person of Jesus with humanity. Jesus must willingly *choose* to lay down his physical life. In His humanity, He must choose to allow the rupture in the relationship with God so that the penalty for sin can be paid. In these ways, God gives self-sacrificially for those He loves, and Jesus tells us that He loves us all (John 3:16).

But, like His peace, God's self-sacrificial love is not given as the world gives it. It has been argued that even in seemingly altruistic self-sacrifice, the sacrificer gets something out of the sacrifice. Ayn Rand is famous for making this argument in her essays in the *Virtue of Selfishness* and other writings. She argues that when we inconvenience ourselves for friends or loved ones, we are getting something in return, whether it is a noble feeling or the strengthening of the relationship. Even in the parent-child relationship, a parent gives to an infant to build a relationship that will later serve the parent in old age. Thus, a seemingly altruistic act really is selfish in that it benefits us, while at the same time benefiting others. Thus, Rand would argue, there is no such thing as selfless altruism and if a person truly does value another's welfare more highly than his or her own, then that person has a serious psychological problem. Rand's argument actually proves more than she intended. It proves the reality of humanity's self-centeredness and God's pure altruism, which confirms Jesus' description of reality.

At Golgotha, God gave His Son as the sacrifice for the sins of the entire world, so that we may be saved from the deserved wrath of God's judgment. God, as the infinite being, having no needs and no deficiencies, does not lack in feelings of nobility. He offers the sacrifice of the cross for one purpose: to have communion with humanity, His creation. God does not do this to remedy a cosmic loneliness. As a triune being, a singular being who exists with internal relationship, He enjoys eternal, perfect community within Himself. The Father and the Son and the Holy Spirit love and interact with one another in an eternal sense. Thus, God does not *need* us for meaningful relationships. Rather, He desires communion with us for its own sake. More to the point, He desires communion with us for *our* sake. He offers that fellowship to us, first by creating us and then by redeeming us, simply out of the boundlessness of His grace. We do not deserve existence, yet He created us. We do not deserve redemption, yet He redeems us. The gift of creation was gracious because it was free. We did not merit it, and it cost God nothing. But the gift of redemption was altruistically loving because it cost God His Son. Love is at its best and most pure when it costs. Jesus paid the infinite cost in securing our relationship with Him. God in Christ is the ultimate expression of the best kind of love—a love that is self-sacrificial.

Sorrow, Justice, and Love at the Place Where They Converge

I always marvel at the way God takes something morbid and dreary and infuses it with meaning and brilliance. God did just that with the once ominous Golgotha. He transformed the Place of the Skull into the place where all three facets of conflict—sorrow, justice, and love—converged and found their resolution.

It is poetic that the very term *crucifixion* has as one of its roots the Latin word *crux*. Crux, which literally means "cross," refers to a pivotal point in resolving an issue. We use it in phrases like, "the *crux* of the issue." We mean, of course, that the crux is at the center of the problem or the issue. More fundamentally, however, is that the crux of anything is the place or point where all the competing and conflicting factors converge. It is at the crux of a matter that the forces in tension with each other collide yet cohere.

The crucifixion of Jesus is the pivotal point of history. There simply is no denying that. The entirety of the Christian faith, which changed the course of history for first-century Palestine, the Roman Empire, and eventually the entire world, has its origin in the reality of Jesus' crucifixion. The historical impact of the crucifixion has been broad and sweeping. But the core of the cross's meaning is in its narrow impact on the spiritual peace of individuals. That specific impact comes from the fact that the three issues we all face in conflict—sorrow, justice, and love—converge and find their resolution at the cross of Jesus Christ.

That narrow and specified impact causes us to reconsider Peter, whom Jesus had once called "Satan" for looking to his own ideas rather than God's about how to resolve the tensions between sorrow, justice, and love. Peter had hoped that Jesus would supernaturally overthrow the Roman oppression and restore righteousness to the religious leadership. Peter had been courageous in the pursuit of that cause and was willing to give his life for it. But as Jesus was being arrested and delivered for crucifixion, Peter's hopes had crumbled. His world became a mass of confusion, and he was not willing to die for that. Instead, he denied even knowing Jesus in order to save his own skin. Thankfully, Peter's story did not end there. Peter himself said that in the days following the crucifixion, the resurrected Jesus appeared to him. Seeing that Jesus had been raised to life, Peter realized that peace came not with the vanquishing of his enemies but with the vanquishing of the curse of sin so that humanity could be reconciled to God. Jesus' resurrection transformed Peter's understanding of what it took for the tensions between sorrow, justice, and love to be resolved.

Sorrow that comes from loss surrounds us and finds its most prevalent and potent manifestation in violent conflict. That sorrow has caused even the most committed believer to ask, "Why?" Or, in the more despondent instances, we can hear amidst the sobs a question that sounds something like, "My God, why have you forsaken me?" The question comes from experiencing the loss of a loved one or something else we hold dear. When we ask God why or believe that He may have forsaken us, we do so because of a deeper loss we fear even more—the loss of our own relationship with God.

When we encounter someone whose heart cries out such questions, do our tongues judge and convict that anguished soul for asking the question, or do we offer him something in his grief? Is it empathy we offer? Unless we have felt sorrow in its most intense forms, empathy remains an abstraction, and we can offer nothing meaningful. What can we offer in the way of understanding to one who has come face to face with such suffering? Can we truly say, "I know what you are going through" when, in fact, we do not? No, we can only embrace the sorrowful soul and say, "I can only imagine what you are going through."

The follower of Jesus can offer something more. The Christian can offer the person of Christ, who suffered the most intense sorrow and anguish that can be imagined. We can offer Jesus as the one who can say, "I know what you are going through." Though He has a divine nature, He knows what it means to have sorrow because of loss. We can turn to Him to bring us through our sorrow, because at Golgotha He had an even more intimate knowledge of sorrow than we. As the Scripture describes Him, He was "a man of sorrows, and acquainted with grief" (Isaiah 53:3 KJV).

Jesus subjected Himself to that sorrow to satisfy the demands of divine justice. As we struggle through the adversity that comes from conflict, we seek satisfaction for our sense of justice. In conflict, we set up battle lines between *us* and *them*. *They* have wronged *us*, and thus *they* must be made to pay. Doubtless, this world is filled with injustice. It is also doubtless that when *they* have wronged *us*, *they* deserve to be punished. But it is equally doubtless that *we* have wronged *them*, and *we* too must pay.

In the administration of human affairs, we must wrestle with these issues and carefully mete out justice where appropriate. We strive for perfect justice because we are made in God's image, having a semblance of His just essence emblazoned on the fleshy tablets of our hearts. But our desire to right wrongs can, and sometimes does, become perverted into mere vengeance. Too often as we seek justice, we forget who God is and who we are. We forget that we have worked injustices on others, and if called to account we would plead for mercy rather than justice. But when we are wronged, we hypocritically call for vengeance. Jesus calls each person to recognize that fallenness in his or her own character. Christ tells us that both *they* and *we* have been unjust and deserve the penalty for those injustices. Jesus eternally paid all of our debts on the cross. Only when we understand this can we begin to fully understand and realize a true and unhypocritical fulfillment of our desire for justice.

Justice demanded a penalty in payment for our sin. Jesus experienced sorrow in paying that penalty. And He paid it for us because of His limitless and pure love.

The desire to receive love is as fundamental as our drive for food. Conflict has a way of depriving us of love. Violent conflict may cause us to lose those closest to us, thereby depriving us of the receipt of their love. Eventually, that deprivation results in an even greater tragedy as our hearts can become stony and brittle, incapable of receiving love or giving love to anyone else. Soon, either numbness or hate, rather than love, dominate our being.

God fulfills our desperate need for the restoration of love lost and saves us from the awful fates of hate and numbness. We desire love because we are relational beings. We—who are the effect—have this relational aspect to our existence because God—who is the cause—is a being in relationship. It would follow, then, that the most powerful drive within the effect is for a relationship with the cause.[23] C. S. Lewis made famous this argument, which has been called the "argument from desire." Lewis posited that for every innate and legitimate desire, there is a fulfillment.

> Creatures are not born with desires unless satisfaction for those desires exists. A baby feels hungry; well, there is such a thing as food. A duckling wants to swim; well, there is such a thing as water. Men feel sexual desire; well, there is such a thing as sex. If I find in myself a desire which no experience in this world can satisfy, the most probable explanation is that I was made for another world.[24]

We feel intense pain in the loss of earthly relationships, especially when such loss is caused by conflict, because the separation of our relationships is a reflection of the more fundamental separation in our relationship with God. That separation is the spiritual separation of our souls from God because of our sin and rebellion. The chasm of separation between humanity and God is infinite because the distance between wickedness and holiness is infinite. At Golgotha, God provided the means to restore that most fundamental relationship between Himself and humanity. In the Cross, where Jesus took on the punishment for our wickedness, the penalty was satisfied and the chasm was bridged. We need only trust that bridge and walk across it.

In other religious systems, we are told that we must build our own bridges by constantly striving to make up for the sins of the past. In those systems, we love God only because of what He can give us if we do enough to earn those rewards or merit forgiveness; thus love is conditional. The Cross demonstrates that what is central to the fundamental gospel is the unconditional relationship between God and humanity. God first loved the world and showed it by giving His Son as the sacrifice for our salvation when we deserved condemnation. That is God's unconditional and perfect love. The Christian has received this love and does not strive to please God in order to get this gift. The Christian does not "give to get" salvation. In fact, because of our fallenness, this is impossible. Rather, the Christian *responds* to God's love in a loving way. Because Jesus achieved our salvation at the cross, we are free now to truly love God for who He is.

Where once we "loved" God to get His gifts, now we love God because He has already given to us. Still, the truly perfect love comes from God, in that He loves us not out of gratitude or obligation. He loves us simply because we exist.

At the Cross, *justice* that required payment for our sin was satisfied.

At the Cross, Jesus endured ineffable *sorrow* in paying that price so that all of this could be accomplished.

At the Cross, God's pure, selfless *love* was expressed in Jesus' willingness to bear the brunt of holy justice by suffering that tremendous sorrow.

Sorrow, justice, and love—the facets of our lives that are the most sharply felt in conflict—collided at the cross. There was no chaos in that collision because justice was served through Jesus' sorrow, which He willingly suffered out of the abundance of His love. At the Place of the Skull, sorrow, justice, and love were harmoniously resolved. In his beautiful hymn, "When I Survey the Wondrous Cross," Isaac Watts reflects on the harmonious collision at the cross.

> When I survey the wondrous cross
> On which the Prince of glory died,
> My richest gain I count but loss,
> And pour contempt on all my pride.
>
> Forbid it, Lord, that I should boast,
> Save in the death of Christ my God!
> All the vain things that charm me most,
> I sacrifice them to His blood.
>
> See from His head, His hands, His feet,
> *Sorrow and love flow mingled down!*
> Did e'er such love and sorrow meet,
> Or thorns compose so rich a crown?
>
> His dying crimson, like a robe,
> Spreads o'er His body on the tree;
> Then I am dead to all the globe,
> And all the globe is dead to me.
>
> Were the whole realm of nature mine,
> That were a present far too small;
> Love so amazing, so divine,
> Demands my soul, my life, my all.[25]

Those suffering from conflict are in need of the hope that there is a resolution to their sorrow, their need for justice, and their desire for love. In Christ, that hope is a reality. It is a reality because in satisfying holy justice, sorrow and love flowed mingled down. But the hope comes not just in the fact that Jesus died at the Place of the Skull, the place where these things converged. The hope comes from the fact that Jesus did not stay dead. The glory of history is found in the truth that Jesus rose from the dead on the third day after His crucifixion. If He had stayed dead, then all we would have is a possibility that a well-meaning man died for what He thought would be our salvation. But the reality of Jesus' resurrection vindicates Jesus' claim that He was laying down His life and raising it up again so that we too could have life. Before His death, Jesus warned His disciples that He would die, but He also encouraged them with the promise that He would live again. He told them that through His death on the cross and His resurrection, those who were once dead in their sin would be alive to God. As only Jesus can do, He summed up the impact of His ministry in but a single sentence: "Because I live, you will live also" (John 14:19).

And through Jesus' work on the cross and His resurrection, we have the assurance that though we are faced with suffering now, in the end, sorrow will end, justice will have its ultimate fulfillment, and Jesus, who is love personified, will fellowship with us forever. G. K. Chesterton expressed the way that this life, filled with so much sorrow, is changed to a life filled with joy when it is redeemed by Christ.

The mass of men have been forced to be gay about the little things, but sad about the big ones. Nevertheless (I offer my last dogma defiantly) it is not native to man to be so. Man is more himself, man is more manlike, when joy is the fundamental thing in him, and grief the superficial. Melancholy should be an innocent interlude, a tender and fugitive frame of mind; praise should be the permanent pulsation of the soul. Pessimism is at best an emotional half-holiday; joy is the uproarious labour by which all things live. Yet, according to the apparent estate of man as seen by the pagan or the agnostic, this primary need of human nature can never be fulfilled. Joy ought to be expansive; but for the agnostic it must be contracted, it must cling to one corner of the world. Grief ought to be a concentration; but for the agnostic its desolation is spread through an unthinkable eternity. This is what I call being born upside down.

Joy, which was the small publicity of the pagan, is the gigantic secret of the Christian.[26]

Jesus promises that joy will become the "gigantic secret" of those who follow Him even though they live in a world wracked with conflict. On the eve of His crucifixion, Jesus told His disciples that soon they would "weep and lament," but their sorrow would "be turned into joy" (John 16:20). Peter's sorrow was so severe that he denied Jesus three times. But his sorrow turned to joy, not just because Jesus rose from the dead, but also because Peter realized that Jesus did not die merely to rise from the dead. He died to resolve the tension between sorrow, justice, and love and to reconcile us to God and give us eternal life. He rose to show us that His death did just that.

The assurance of that eternal life results in something much greater than happiness. It results in joy, which lingers beyond a mere moment. Joy lingers beyond happiness because when we are joyous, we have peace about the future and the sanctity and permanence of a relationship with God. Hundreds of years before Jesus' birth, the prophet Isaiah prophesied that the Messiah's suffering from violence would bring us that kind of peace,

He was pierced because of our transgressions, crushed because of our iniquities; *punishment for our peace was on Him.* (Isa. 53:5 HCSB, emphasis added)

In a vacuum, Isaiah's statement is strange and mysterious. But in the context of the greatest act in history, where sorrow, justice, and love harmoniously converged, we understand how Jesus' suffering brings us peace—a peace that can overflow to the world around us.

Chapter 6

RIPPLES AND REFLECTIONS

The Supremacy of Jesus Christ

The vertical peace between God and humanity is the crucial first stage in the realization of true peace. The second stage is the horizontal reconciliation within and between humanity that results from the first stage. Calling the vertical reconciliation the "first" stage seems to imply that it ends or that its primacy ceases when the second stage begins. But that is far from the truth. The truth is that lasting reconciliation among people is possible only when people have lasting reconciliation with God. Both the vertical reconciliation between God and humanity and the horizontal reconciliation within the human race began at the Cross. Even more fundamental than that, however, is that both kinds of reconciliation find their origin and their eternality at the Cross. The first stage, our reconciliation to God, does not end or have less meaning when the second stage, our reconciliation to each other, begins. Rather, the second stage emanates from the first. In other words, the permanence of the first stage is the very thing that sustains the persistence of the second.

Conflict has permanence in our world when we ignore the Cross, when we forget that we are all equal at the Cross. When

that happens, the reconciliation that came from that foundation crumbles into so much rubble. One might think that the
intangible rubble of ruined reconciliation is a metaphor for the
tangible rubble of bombed-out buildings and homes that are
the hallmarks of war and conflict. May I suggest that the opposite is true? The rubble of homes and buildings destroyed by
shelling and gunfire is the physical shadow of the real spiritual ruin that occurs when we forget the vertical reconciliation between God and man that comes from the cross and only
from the cross.

Let us look at a different physical metaphor to better understand the spiritual interplay between the vertical and horizontal reconciliations. Think of a hailstone that falls into a
pond of calm, still water. The hailstone impacts the pond with
downward, vertical force. That impact is most intense at the
initial point of impact, but the effect is not confined just to that
initial point. The effect is not just superficial. There is something explosive happening below the surface as the hailstone
plummets through the water, displacing it and causing it to
stir. There is also an outward force from the vertical impact.
The outward force creates ripples in the once calm surface of
the pond. As the displaced water below the surface churns, it
collides with the outward force. Ripples are created in the water that quickly spread.

In much the same way, God intersected human history in
the vertical sense in the incarnation of Jesus Christ. That vertical intersection had an explosive ripple effect in the immediate area of the community in which Jesus walked, preached,
and healed. But it was Jesus' crucifixion that punctuated the
vertical impact of God's incarnation and caused the spirit of
man to churn by providing the means for reconciliation between humanity and God. His resurrection from the dead so-
lidified that vertical impact for all time.

The horizontal effect from God's vertical impact on humanity is no less profound. The solid record of history has demonstrated that Jesus' effect on the course of human events was

not confined to a small Middle Eastern community in the first century. The ripple effects of God's impact on human history in the person and work of Christ have been felt the whole world over and for more than two thousand years. Those emanating ripples are particularly appropriate to our examination of the kind of peace that the gospel provides. It is to the second and horizontal stage of reconciliation, perpetuated by the deep impact of the first, that we now turn.

The Cycle of Divine Reflection

Playing with and teaching my children has blessed me with one of the subtle joys of parenthood, namely, the recovery of the ability to delight in the minutiae of life. When I was a child, it took only the words, "Once upon a time" to stir my imagination in anticipation of more to come. As an adult, my sensitivity to such delight has waned a bit. But I have found that as I watch my children grow, learn, and explore the immense world before them, I regain that childlike sense again, if only vicariously and if only for a moment. Ravi Zacharias has called this phenomenon "recapturing the wonder" in his wonderful book by that name. I now find myself recapturing the wonder and making much ado about even the smallest of my kids' achievements, and my joy in those small victories seems to last forever. When my son first began to read, I asked him to do it over and over, just as he would repeatedly exclaim, "Again!" each time I tossed him into the air.

My son, who is three years old at the time of this writing, continually surprises me with how acutely aware he is of my every word and action. He loves to watch cartoons with me. My wife would laugh and think to herself that I probably like to watch the cartoons more than my son (which is probably true). I experience one of the small heartbreaks of fatherhood whenever my son asks me to watch cartoons or play with him at times when I have to lock myself in my home office to write or conduct research. "I can't play now," I tell him. "I have a lot of work to do on the computer." I tell him that occasionally, and, occasionally, he will accept that answer. But looking at his disappointed face, I simply must tell him, "But after I work, then cartoons!"

A few months ago, we were eating lunch together in the kitchen on a Saturday, and I asked my son, "When we get done with our lunch, do you want to watch cartoons with me?"

"Not right now," he answered. "I have a lot of work to do on the computer."

I was simultaneously astonished and deflated. Within minutes, I learned that what he meant by "a lot of work to do on the computer" was that he wanted to play the children's video games on our computer. As I was taking in what he had just said to me, he followed it up with another zinger. He pointed at me as if he was the father and I was his son and said, "But after I finish my work, then cartoons, okay?" I did not know whether to be disappointed or delighted.

Every parent knows the joys (and sometimes the horrors) of witnessing our little ones repeat something we have said or mimic our actions. This shows us that there is something instinctual within us that drives us to emulate those we admire or those we perceive to be in a higher station than we are in. Infants and toddlers imitate their parents; teenagers imitate famous musicians, actors, or athletes; adults mimic and aspire to be like other adults they admire.

May I suggest that this instinct to imitate transcends obvious social dynamics and actually shapes our spiritual lives as well. Think of the philosophies and religions prevalent throughout human history. Many such worldviews look to a formal deity or even a pantheon of deities as the giver or givers of divine guidance and commands for humanity. Islam looks to the will of Allah, revealed in the Qur'an, as that which is to be submitted to, and looks to Muhammad and other prophets as examples of those who have properly submitted to that will. Some strands of Hinduism look to a multiplicity of gods and goddesses who each govern some aspect of existence and give us divine instructions and examples. Some deities exemplify love, others compassion, others money, and still others destruction. Even worldviews that do not necessarily espouse the existence of a personal deity look to some kind of exemplar for morality and behavior. For example, Buddhism, which in its traditional form does not recognize a formal deity, has come to exalt its founder, Siddhartha Gautama, or even the bodhisattvas, the figures in Buddhist history who have attained "enlightenment." Tibetan Buddhism sees the Dalai Lama as the incarnation of the bodhisattva of compassion. Even secular humanism and atheism look to humanity as the ultimate authority on meaning and morality. The Humanist Manifesto III affirms that humanity has the "ability and responsibility to lead ethical lives of personal fulfillment that aspire to the greater good of humanity."[1]

Every worldview, then, looks to some kind of ultimate exemplar for human morality and interaction. In most worldviews, the exemplars are the central deities, while in other worldviews, the best of the species are the exemplars. The wills and actions of those exemplars, and their moral characters and qualities, are to be emulated and followed to the greatest extent possible. Every worldview, to some degree or another, teaches its practitioners to live in peace and harmony with one another when possible. Though the effectiveness or consistency (or even coherency) of this teaching in some worldviews is a matter of debate, the fact remains that every worldview tries to teach this message in some fashion. Since humans imitate those in authority or those who are perceived to be at a higher level of some kind, it is not a worldview's wooden edicts to love each other that people follow; rather the moral example of a worldview's particular deity or avatar or leader has the greatest influence on people's interactions with one another.

In most religions that espouse a deity, the deity demands that we act in a certain way or by a certain code to attain the deity's favor and obtain the ultimate goal of existence as defined by that religion. In Islam, salvation comes when a Muslim believes in God and does enough good works to outweigh his evil deeds.[2] In Hinduism, one can break free from the cycle of reincarnation and become one with *Brahman*, the impersonal reality of the universe, only after fully working through one's *karma*—the effects of deeds in past lives—by doing good deeds in our numerous reincarnations. Buddhism is similar, in that one can break free from repeated reincarnation by ridding oneself of desire and following the Eightfold Path—right views, right aspiration, right speech, right conduct, right livelihood, right effort, right mindfulness, and right contemplation.

Even those who do not specifically ascribe to a religious system often follow "divine" moral ethics for salvation. Indeed, although it is something of an oversimplification, it has been correctly observed that many people believe in a variation of "Good Personism": If you live a good life, you will go to heaven. In the humanist or atheist paradigm, good personism is defined this way: If we all live the good lives we are capable of living, we can create heaven on earth. Whether we strive for nirvana, heaven, moksha, or utopia, we can attain them only if we do something or give something first. Thus, whether religious or secular, each of these worldviews has at its center a quality that can be characterized as conditional. More to the point, I think it can be fairly said that these worldviews and their respective exemplars are *demanding*. The ultimate authorities demand something from the followers. Obedience, effort, worship, sacrifice, and appeasement are commanded and demanded as the conditions one must satisfy for salvation. Or, in naturalistic frameworks, nature rewards only the strong. The ultimate authorities in such worldviews do not give freely in that sense. They demand our resources from us in exchange for their favor and good gifts.

All worldviews have a reflective character about them. We reflect the attributes of what we worship. That is to say, just as children imitate their parents, the adherents of a particular worldview will emulate the words and deeds of their chosen deities or exemplars. If we follow a demanding deity, our actions and character will reflect that characteristic. Given humanity's penchant for imitation, it seems intuitive that if our deities or avatars are demanding of us, we too will be demanding of each other. This demanding quality creates multifaceted tensions and conflicts for humanity. We struggle with the tension of hoarding commodities to ourselves, while feeling the guilt of not giving over to our deities that which they require of us. There are only so many resources, and if we give those up to the divine or to society, what will be left for us? But the fact that the divine or ultimate authorities demand resources from us leads to horizontal types of conflicts. As we imitate the ultimate authorities in our worldviews, we too demand resources. The competition for resources is one of the principle causes of conflict in the world. We compete for land, for money, for natural resources, and for power. There are only so many of these resources to go around, and sometimes we feel it necessary to take them by force or to use force to keep others from taking them from us. Thus, conflict is born.

The paradigm of conflict based on competition for resources is the logical outworking of—indeed the driving force behind— the purely naturalistic, atheistic view of the world. In that worldview, chance is the creator of all things, and fairness is random. Also ultimately random is who has resources, who does not, who has the power to take them, and who is powerless to stop others from taking them. Genetic chance may allow for one group to rise up and better compete with other groups for resources. "Survival of the fittest" is the end game, which really equates to the maxim "might makes right." In the naturalistic framework, there is no logically compelling reason for humanity to be exempt from this maxim. If chance is our father and nature is red in tooth and claw, then humanity that has forsaken the supernatural for the purely natural will reflect the teachings of its maker.

There is a cyclical quality to this reflective paradigm. We reflect the characteristics of what we worship. But where we create false gods, it is equally true that the characteristics of the deities we create reflect our characteristics. When the ancients created gods of love, gods of sexuality, gods of war, gods of destruction, gods of creation, gods of fertility, gods of mischief, and gods of compassion, they were creating deities that reflected human characteristics and human fickleness. Mythologies and sacred texts of other faiths tell us of capricious, mischievous, and deceptive gods who competed with one another and played games with humanity. Such characteristics reflected human fallenness, not holiness. In the generations following the institution of such idolatry, humanity re-reflected the values of the gods it created. And so the cycle goes on: man creates gods imitating man's image, then man imitates the words and deeds of the graven images he has created. The image of a mirror held in front of another mirror comes to mind. As they reflect each other, an infinite regression of successively smaller reflections can be seen. It is little wonder that as humanity traps itself in the cycle of imitating its artificial deities, our selfishness increases, the value of human life regressively decreases, and we inflict suffering on each other through conflict.

Is Christianity any different that it might offer us solutions? If we look at isolated passages in the Old Testament, we might be tempted to think that it is not. The very first of the Ten Commandments tells us that we must have no other gods beside Yahweh Elohim (Exod. 20:3). In the Old Testament, we see God striking people dead and judging entire nations for worshiping other gods. In fact, God says of Himself that he is a "jealous God" (Exod. 20:5; 34:14; Deut. 4:24; 5:9; Josh. 24:19).

It is important to take the Bible at its word on this point and fully embrace the fact that Christianity espouses that God is "jealous." But it is equally important to understand the biblical view of God's jealousy in the context of His ultimate selflessness. God is "jealous" (some English translations say He is "zealous") for His holy name, which is to say that He fervently protects the sanctity and specialness of His identity and integrity. He will not allow it to be compromised by permitting

His people to follow after false gods, which really are no gods at all.

Paradoxically, in God's zealousness there is a selflessness that looks after our welfare. Throughout the Old Testament accounts, God brings judgment upon His people for violating His will and for looking to pieces of wood or molded metal, or even themselves, for ultimate answers. God knows that there is no help in these invented saviors. There is only destruction and pettiness because destructive and petty people created them. God knows that when man creates deities for himself, or even makes himself into a deity, only the destructive cycle of imitation follows.

There is yet another reason for God's zealous protection of His identity and relationship with us. His people were the progenitors of Jesus, through whom the true divine help and redemption for humanity would come. Through God's people, Jesus would be born; God incarnate would save the world from itself. By judging and condemning the actions of those who would attribute saving power to powerless beings or nonbeings, God was keeping His people from putting their trust in the untrustworthy. He safeguarded the Messiah's legacy so that when He came, died for our sins, and rose again, there would be a community of believers to propagate the message and perpetuate the account of God's self-giving and selfless love expressed on the cross.

Therein lies a uniqueness of the Christian worldview. Christianity is different because it is demonstrable that man did not create the God of the Bible in man's image. From the splendor and design of creation to the strong historical case for Jesus' resurrection, we have ample reason to be confident that the God of the Bible eternally preexisted humanity and made us in His image. But there is another clue to show us that we did not create Yahweh.

Humanity creates its deities in its own image. Yet the God of the Bible is very different from us. In no other worldview do we find the teaching that the one and only Creator of the universe also gives of Himself. The cycle of reflection that exists in other worldviews is absent from the Christian faith. We did not create Yahweh to reflect our values and then teach our children to reflect the values of our own creation. It is God who created us to reflect His splendor and His attributes.

When it comes to putting an end to the self-centeredness that gives birth to conflict, there is no deity who is better to reflect than the only actual deity, the God of the Bible. Indeed, God in Christ is the very embodiment of selflessness, in contradistinction to the selfishness we see all around us. God Himself came in the person of Jesus to commune with us so that we could better understand Him. Thus, in the incarnation itself God was self-giving. And as I have stated in previous chapters, in the act of willingly going to the cross to suffer the punishment we deserved, God was ultimately self-giving.

As He is described in the Bible, God is the one who communes with us through His Holy Spirit. He has revealed Himself to be a being of pure love. If it is true that we imitate those in authority, then when we commit ourselves to reflecting God's self-giving nature, we commit ourselves to ending the selfishness that is the mother of conflict.

Imperfect Reflections

But what about the Crusades? What about the Inquisition? What about those Western Christians who once owned slaves? Are these not monstrous episodes of Christians reflecting the attributes of the God they claim to follow? Do these historical examples give the lie to the argument that we should imitate and follow the example of the God of the Bible?

We have dealt partially with this quite natural and fair question in the previous chapter. To some extent (but I would argue to an exaggerated extent) it is true that those claiming to be Christians have wrought substantial evil and suffering across history. There are many great works discussing the extent to which such charges are true or false, so I will not dwell on the details here. Suffice it to say, however, that such ugly episodes are hardly perfect reflections of the character of the God of the Bible. Far from it, they are gross distortions of His character. Of course, anyone can make that argument in defense of his or her worldview. The proof of that defense lies in looking at the central teachings of the worldview, and most especially at the character of the founder. With regard to the Christian faith, a number of questions arise. Is there a teaching of Jesus that we can look to that is consistent with the horrors of the Inquisition? Where does Jesus teach us that we must take the Holy Land back by force? Where does He tell us that we must force others to believe as we do? Where does Jesus teach us to hate or kill our enemies? Where does Jesus tell us that one race is superior to another? We will be hard-pressed to find any such teachings or actions that would suggest that Jesus espoused such things.

Indeed, Christ preached nothing but the opposite of hate when He told His followers to love their enemies.

> You have heard that it was said, "You shall love your neighbor and hate your enemy." But I say to you, love your enemies and pray for those who persecute you, so that you may be sons of your Father who is in heaven; for He causes His sun to rise on the evil and the good, and sends rain on the righteous and the unrighteous. For if you love those who love you, what reward do you have? Do not even the tax collectors do the same? If you greet only your brothers, what more are you doing than others? (Matt. 5:43–47 NASB)

The point should be clear. Christians acting horribly are not acting consistently with Jesus' teaching or His actions. They are acting inconsistently with them. They are not perfectly reflecting the selflessness of God in Christ; they are reflecting God's image as a funhouse mirror grotesquely distorts whatever it reflects.

Philip Yancey has dealt with the topic of the moral failings of institutionalized religion. He notes that G. K. Chesterton readily admitted that the church had failed the gospel.[3] Rather than seeing these failings as a strike against Christianity, however, Chesterton found them to be a proof that Christianity's teaching that human beings are fallen creatures is true. Yancey points out that Chesterton argued that the failure of Christians is "one of the strongest arguments in favor of Christianity," because their failure proves what Christianity teaches about the Fall and the doctrine of original sin.[4] According to Yancey, Chesterton rightly points out that humanity gone wrong proves that the Bible is right.[5]

Is there really any need for proof that what is amiss with human-driven peace efforts is humanity itself? I was trained as an attorney. Practicing law is often a challenging and stimulating profession. It involves the analysis of complex legal issues in light of increasingly complicated facts and the diverse interests of clients. There is the need to strategize and consider the tactical aspects of a case. These are the enjoyable parts of the legal profession. The practice of law has many downsides, however. I recall a time when I sat next to another attorney during a break in a rather contentious negotiation involving multiple parties. During the brief respite, he slumped in his chair and said half in jest and half in truth, "You know, this would be a great job if it weren't for other attorneys, their clients, our clients, witnesses, and juries." Later, as I was fighting traffic to get home after that frustrating day, I extended his sentiments to the mass of commuters who also were just trying to get home. *Human existence would be wonderful if it weren't for other human beings.*

Humanity suffers from something of a species-wide bipolar disorder. We simultaneously think both very much and very little of ourselves. We spend thousands of dollars fueling the campaigns of politicians running for office, yet once they are elected we spend our time and energy complaining about and distrusting them. We ask the clergy to officiate at our weddings, yet we cynically suspect that they are really only after our money. We protest military actions, but we tie yellow ribbons around our mailboxes showing support for our troops. Though we are complex, inconsistent beings, we still look to ourselves to engineer a better future and a peaceful existence.

In secular humanism, unreliable humanity is humanity's best choice for deliverance for the simple reason that there is no other choice. Yet we find ourselves perpetually frustrated when we break our own promises, when countries repeatedly violate treaties and accords, and when one culture persists in its hatred of another. I once read a humorous quote on a refrigerator magnet that speaks to humanity's vacillations.

> As a rule, a man's a fool;
> When it's hot, he wants it cool;
> When it's cool, he wants it hot;
> Always wanting what is not.

Despite our evident inconsistency and unreliability, we continue to put our faith in "the goodness of man," while forgetting the old truism that *even the best of men are at best just men.*

Misplaced religiosity fares no better than secularism in this regard. In the history of religion, we can see that we have created deities that act as inconsistently as we do, with moral shortcomings that mirror our own. Our self-created deities are fickle and hot-tempered, and so we are fickle and hot-tempered. Though our false gods are inconsistent in their demands, they are consistently demanding. And so we are as well. I once saw a tee shirt with a quote that read, "God save me from your followers." It is a sarcastic dig at organized religions in general that does not attack any particular religion. Strangely, though, it tries to point out that religious adherents act in ways that harm others. It goes further, perhaps, in saying that the very idea of God leads to harmful behavior. So I do not fully agree with its point, as it is a blatant overstatement. But there is

some truth in it. The gods that many people in the world follow
are a reflection of humanity's less desirable traits. Humanity
re-reflects those same traits.

Revisiting the Ripples

If humanity and religion fail us when we seek the solution
to human conflict, where, then, can we look for the answer?
What is the true image that we can look to and reflect? In the
gospel message, we find God to be selfless and self-sacrificing
in His love for humanity. In paying for our sins on the cross,
He does for us what we cannot do for ourselves, and He does
it though we do not deserve it. In the Christian faith, the one
who accepts this gift experiences a transformation in his life
from the divine. Embracing the God who gives so selflessly
changes the follower of Christ from a self-centered being to a
selfless being. This is one effect of what the Scripture refers to
as *sanctification*. It is a process by which the Holy Spirit floods
the life of one who has put his or her trust in Christ and transforms that life. Through the sanctifying process, the believer
is changed over time from a funhouse mirror that only vaguely
reflects the divine *imago Dei* to a true reflection of Christ's
character. To be sure, the follower of Christ still sins and will
sometimes consider personal interests before the interests of
others. But the sanctification process gradually (and in many
cases suddenly and dramatically) metamorphoses a believer
from a self-consumed being to one who is concerned for others.
Jesus refers to the beginning of the process as being "born
again" spiritually (John 3:3, 5–7). Paul refers to this transformation as becoming a "new creation" (2 Cor. 5:17).

This is the individualized and vertical impact of Jesus' gospel on each life. But the impact is not localized to the individual follower of Christ. We are social creatures by nature.
When Christ transforms an individual's selfish nature into
being others-centered, that "new creation" becomes more positively influential in the community and Christ becomes more

attractive to others. It follows, then, that the population of that community becomes that much more others-centered. As we saw in chapter 3, the transformation in the Samaritan woman at Jacob's well was infectious and influenced a community-wide change of hearts (John 4). If conflict is born out of human competition for resources, then a community that is not interested in hoarding resources but is intent on spreading resources for the betterment of all becomes the agent for peace on earth. Instead of competing for resources with others and instead of fighting to keep the resources we have, the community of those who follow Christ should strive to spread the wealth. This is true of material resources, of course. But the most important resource one person can offer another—indeed the resource that never depletes and is itself contagious—is the peace of reconciliation to God through the love of Christ. In other worldviews we suffer from the impure reflections and re-reflections of our deities and ourselves, but that cycle is broken in Christ. God is the selfless moral exemplar as demonstrated at the Place of the Skull. When our sanctification causes us to reflect God's selflessness, we are on the road toward more perfectly reflecting the original *imago Dei* as God intended.

It has been argued that with socialism and communism humanity already has experimented with this kind of social selflessness and failed. Communism and socialism failed as human endeavors because they are fatally flawed in their fundamental assumptions. They both posit that humanity, unaided by spiritual regeneration, can be trusted to overcome its selfishness and create its own utopia. Their other fatal flaw is that the state legislates and enforces some form of selflessness. While secular humanism does not necessarily espouse the legislation of selflessness, it suffers from the flawed assumption that humanity is capable of self-actualizing selflessness. If the failures of communism, socialism, and secular humanism have proved anything, it is that we are incapable of achieving a true selflessness apart from a Spirit-dominated, regenerated nature that reflects the selflessness, not of the creation, but of the Creator.

We return now to the metaphor of the pond. When a single hailstone strikes the surface of the water, the resultant ripples spread across the water, but their strength diminishes with distance. The kinetic energy dissipates as it is absorbed in the surface tension of the pond. The ripples thus fail to affect the entire pond. Now imagine, not just a single hailstone, but a hailstorm descending on the pond. Each hailstone has its own vertical impact. Each energy-less spot in the water suddenly bursts with activity. Each vertical impact creates its own ripple effect. Quickly, the ripples from one hailstone crash into the ripples from another. The once stagnant pond quickly becomes alive. Its entire surface dances with the horizontal effects of the many vertical impacts.

As Christ intersects the stagnant waters of each of our lives, there is an immediate vertical effect—the deep and profound impact of a life changed by reconciliation to God. As the depth of that experience is explored and we understand more fully what it means for Jesus to be the incarnation of the eternal God and the selfless sacrifice for our sins, we begin to understand true selflessness. We have a greater understanding of what it means to have an impact on others, including those who are at odds with us, or those we would call enemies. But there is only so much one person can do for the world. The ripples of that person's efforts are still felt and still spread, but they diminish as the energy is swallowed up by the immensity of the human collective.

A hailstorm of the kind of selflessness that emanates from the believer who emulates Christ is needed to affect the entire pond of human existence. Christ commissions each one of us who professes faith in Him to contribute to the hailstorm of reconciliation in two ways. One way is to act selflessly toward others so that they may see our good works and look to God as their source (Matt. 5:16). This readies the souls of others to receive the most important commodity we can offer—Jesus Christ Himself. The second way we can contribute is by telling others of the selfless God we serve. In fact, Jesus commissions us to do this (see Matt. 28:19–20). Though the follower of Christ will sometimes fall far short of this selfless ideal, there remains a contagiousness to divinely inspired selflessness because there is a contagiousness to Jesus. One life vertically impacted by Jesus creates a horizontal ripple effect that impacts others. As the gospel is shared with and accepted by others, a hailstorm gathers and descends on the stagnation of humanity. A maelstrom ensues, and the lifelessness of a selfish world can be transformed into the teaming furor of a community of the selfless.

The apostle Paul beautifully describes the horizontal result of God's vertical impact in our lives through Christ.

> Therefore, if anyone is in Christ, there is a new creation; old things have passed way, and look, new things have come. Now everything is from God, who reconciled us to Himself through Christ and gave us the ministry of reconciliation: that is, in Christ, God was reconciling the world to Himself, not counting their trespasses against them, and He has committed the message of reconciliation to us. Therefore, we are ambassadors for Christ; certain that God is appealing through us, we plead on Christ's behalf, "Be reconciled to God." He made the One who did not know sin to be sin for us, so that we might become the righteousness of God in Him. (2 Cor. 5:17–21 HCSB)

Paul says that when we have been reconciled to God through Christ (the first part of the vertical impact), we become the righteousness of God (the second part of the vertical impact). We are commissioned to be ambassadors for Christ to others (the horizontal impact), so that they, too, might become the righteousness of God.

The core cause of conflict is the selfish competition for resources. In a community of the selfless, we no longer compete to acquire resources; we compete with each other in trying to give them away. We do this, not because the human-driven state legislates such activity from without, but because the Holy Spirit impels from within us to act this way. Thus, we reflect a selflessness and a love that initiates rather than reacts.

> Beloved, let us love one another, for love is from God; and everyone who loves is born of God and knows God. The one who does not love does not know God, for God is love. By this the love of God was manifested in us, that God has sent His only begotten Son into the world so that we might live through Him. In this is love, not that we loved God, but that He loved us and sent His Son *to be* the propitiation for our sins. Beloved, if God so loved us, we also ought to love one another. (1 John 4:7–11 NASB)

At the risk of mixing my metaphors, allow me to point out the poetic paradox in our reflection of the divine selflessness found in God's incarnation. It is this: completely still waters reflect an image far more accurately than tumultuous waters, yet the selfless God revealed in the Gospels is inaccurately reflected when humanity is spiritually still. God's character is best reflected when we actively reach out in love and cause a stir within the pool of humanity.

Through the gift of salvation, God has resolved our longing for love and restored the lost relationship by giving us something better than worldly love. He has given us unmerited love so that we might impart our own love to those who do not merit it, even those we perceive as enemies. As it spreads, it ultimately leads to national and international reconciliation among even ancient and fierce enemies. Some 2,700 years ago, the prophet Isaiah made a specific prophecy about God's ability to reconcile the world to Himself and then the world to itself. Isaiah presciently wrote that the Egyptians and the Assyrians, Israel's ancient and great enemies, would be reconciled. In fact, the prophecy God gave to Isaiah shows us that

God uses suffering to bring these great nations, along with the Israelites, to Himself.

> In that day, there will be a highway from Egypt to Assyria, and the Assyrians will come into Egypt and the Egyptians into Assyria, and the Egyptians will worship with the Assyrians. In that day Israel will be the third party with Egypt and Assyria, a blessing in the midst of the earth, whom the LORD of hosts has blessed, saying, "Blessed is Egypt My people, and Assyria the work of My hands, and Israel My inheritance." (Isa. 19:23–25 NASB)

Egypt, the nation that spawned Hagar, whose son Ishmael is the father of the Arabs, will be reconciled to Israel. Assyria, the progenitor of many Arab countries, also will be reconciled to Israel. Is that not an astounding and audacious prediction? But what will be the character of this reconciliation? The character is quite obvious: these nations will all be servants and adopted children of the Most High God. They will be reconciled because they will all be God's people. The Lord of Hosts calls Egypt "My people" just as He called Israel His people. Assyria is the work of His hands and Israel is His inheritance.

But how can this reconciliation be? What is there that can unite Egypt, Assyria, and Israel? Economic equality? Managed borders? Cease-fires? Such measures may help in part, but they are fleeting and temporary because they are only bandages on an infected wound. The bleeding may be temporarily stopped, but the sickness continues to kill the body. Is the cure for the sickness to be found in winning the debate over theories of the end times or in supporting any one group because of the vicissitudes of genetics? Quite the opposite has happened, actually.

No, the answer comes to us from the Jew, the Christian, the Roman citizen, and the world traveler—the apostle Paul. History tells us that Paul, once called Saul of Tarsus, was so violently opposed to the new "Way" that he sought to destroy the burgeoning church. As both Christian and non-Christian historians recognize, however, Paul was changed in a moment after having what he testified to as a real encounter with the risen Lord. And it was this Paul who recognized that peace comes, not through social engineering and foreign policy, but through the person of Christ.

> *For He is our peace*, who made both groups one and tore down the dividing wall of hostility. In His flesh, He did away with the law of the commandments in regulations, so that He might create in Himself one new man from the two, resulting in peace. He did this so that He might reconcile both to God in one body through the cross and put the hostility to death by it. (Eph. 2:14–16 HCSB, emphasis added)

This echoes Paul's words in Galatians 3:28–29 that in Christ, no one is given a special place or deprived of a special place because of race, gender, or economic or social status. All are one in Christ and can have the assurance of being equal "heirs according to the promise." What can make Arabs, Jews, and all others into one spiritual people are our common need to be rescued from ourselves and the common availability of that rescue found in Christ.

Christianity is unique, not because it offers a clever "method" or "way of life" to obtain peace within humanity. Christianity is unique because it offers a person, Jesus Christ, as the one through whom we can have peace first with God and then with each other. It is unique because it offers Jesus, who Himself "is our peace." We find it difficult to follow isolated or abstract rules for good conduct without an example to follow. In other words, we more accurately and effectively follow people rather than rules. An accurate reflection of the holy is much more difficult—in fact, impossible—when the divine cannot be approached or remains just an abstract concept. But the reflection becomes so much easier to actualize when God approaches us in the embodiment of the incarnation and makes Himself known in the most intimate of ways. Perhaps this is in part what Jesus conveyed when He declared that His yoke is easy and His burden is light (Matt. 11:30). But there is something more there. Jesus did not come with a new set of moral codes, nor did He come merely to exemplify God's moral standard for us. He came to do much more. As I have heard it famously said, "Jesus did not come to make bad people good; He came to make dead people live."[6]

Try as I might, I cannot summarize Jesus' mission any better than that. Without Christ, we are spiritually dead, both to God and to each other. Only after being raised to life, having our sins forgiven and our souls reconciled to God, can we begin to have peace. Through Jesus, we are made alive and peace becomes possible. Through Him, each one of us can have resolution of the tensions between sorrow, justice, and love that emanate from conflict. When we have that resolved within ourselves, we are free to offer that resolution to others. Jesus, and Jesus alone, has broken down the dividing wall that prevented that freedom. That freedom leads to one final facet of the power of the gospel that we shall explore next—the power of transformation.

Chapter 7

AND NOW THESE THREE REMAIN

Transforming Sorrow,
Justice, and Love

The First Transformation

Years ago on a cold and cloudy November day, I received the worst news I had ever heard. It was my freshman year of college, and I was away from home at the University of Buffalo. I was attending there on a full basketball scholarship, with dreams of being in the starting lineup of a Division I NCAA basketball program. My dream had been to play basketball at the University of Michigan, but the year I was recruited out of high school, the University of Michigan managed to sign every single one of their top recruits.[1]

I had come back to my dorm room from my morning classes for a nap. As I lay in my bed, I had trouble falling asleep. I was thinking about my family and my future and just could not quiet my mind enough to doze off. As I was trying to relax, the phone rang, which was unusual; I rarely received calls in the middle of the day because everyone I knew was either in class or at work. Hearing the phone ring in the late morning, I had an immediate sense that something was wrong.

I picked up the phone to hear the voice of Sumi, a high school

friend of mine who had stayed in Michigan to attend college.
"Hi, Abdu. It's Sumi."

"Hi, Sumi. Long time no talk. How are things back in Michigan?" I asked.

"Things are okay. Hey, I'm calling because I just caught the local news, and I saw a story about the attempted robbery of a jewelry store in Hamtramck."

My heart immediately sank. A few years before, my father had opened a jewelry store in Hamtramck, Michigan, and he was doing quite well. Although there were many other jewelry stores in that city, something inside me was beginning to panic at the thought that a jewelry store in the area was on the news.

"There are lots of jewelry stores in Hamtramck," I said pensively. "Did they say the name of the store that was robbed?" I still held onto the hope that it had only been a robbery—some items were taken and nothing more. But I was wrong.

"I didn't catch the name," he responded. "But the news said that two brothers who work there had been shot. I thought I'd give you a call because I remember you once told me that your uncle works with your dad at the store."

I could not speak. Before he had even finished his sentence, I began to prepare myself for the worst. There were plenty of jewelry stores in Hamtramck, and most were family owned, so the victims could be any of a number of people. In the cacophony of worried thoughts, I was suddenly sickened by the realization that I was holding out hope that someone other than my father and uncle had been shot. Yet I was becoming more certain that my family was going to be profoundly changed forever.

After a pause, I stammered a response. "Sumi, thanks for calling. I'm going to call home. I'll let you know what I find out." I immediately hung up, but I did not call home for a few minutes. My mind was racing far too much for me to talk to anyone. I was hundreds of miles away from my family and friends. I had no one to immediately turn to for comfort. So I took a few minutes to prepare myself for whatever news I might get from home. Maybe it was another jewelry store; maybe my father and uncle were perfectly fine. But maybe they were not. I paced my dorm room for a few minutes. The tension and uncertainty mounted. I went out into the hallway. I came back into my room. I went to the window, opened it, and drew in a deep breath of the crisp November air.

At last I was sufficiently calm enough to start dialing my parents' home number. The answering machine picked up with my mother's voice. "You have reached the Murray residence. We're not available to take your call, but if you leave a message after the tone, we'll get back to you." Usually, the sound of her voice comforted me—even if it was only a recorded greeting. But the fact that she had not answered the phone that particular morning made the tinny-sounding recording of her voice disquieting.

The answering machine recorded messages digitally, so I could always tell how many messages were on the machine by how long it took for the beeps following the recorded greeting to stop sounding. The more beeps from the machine, the more unanswered messages it had recorded. I was praying that there would not be many beeps. But there were. In fact, there seemed to be endless beeps. As I heard each one, it became clear that my parents' phone had been flooded with calls that morning. That could mean only one thing. It was my father and my uncle who had been shot.

But I still held out hope that maybe they hadn't. Maybe the messages were from people like Sumi, who had seen the news story and had called my mother just to make sure my father and uncle were okay. Maybe my mother was out shopping and hadn't had a chance to return the phone calls yet. My mother did not have a cell phone (they were not as common then as they are today). I called my grandmother at her home, but she did not answer. I called another uncle, but he did not answer. I called my cousins, but they did not answer. I had run out of options—except for one. I could call my father's store and find out the truth quickly and directly.

But I hesitated.

If something had happened, who would pick up the phone? Some stranger? A police officer? Maybe my father would answer and tell me all was well. How would I react if someone I did not know answered the phone and told me the worst news I could possibly hear? But I had to find out, so I stirred up my courage and dialed the number.

My uncle, who owned a restaurant down the street, answered.

Hearing his voice, I knew something had happened to my father and other uncle because he rarely visited the store back then. "Amu?" I said. (*Amu* means "uncle" in Arabic.) "A friend of mine in Michigan called me and said that two brothers were shot in a jewelry store robbery in Hamtramck. Is everyone okay?"

"I don't want you to get too upset," he answered in an effort to keep me calm. "Your dad and your uncle are at the hospital, and they'll be okay. But your dad was shot in the stomach and your uncle was shot in the shoulder." He tried his best to sound confident in what he was telling me, but I could tell that he had no assurance that they would be okay. He continued, "Your mom and the rest of the family are at the hospital. Don't try to drive home. We'll get you a flight home as soon as possible."

I had been preparing myself for that very news, but it still floored me. I mumbled some kind of response to my uncle and got off the phone. Somehow we managed to arrange a flight from Buffalo to Detroit that evening. I vividly remember the ensuing hours between that phone call with my uncle and my boarding the flight to Detroit. I walked from my dorm room at the University of Buffalo's Ellicott Complex to the Alumni Arena, where the basketball team practiced and played. Finding no escape from my worst thoughts and fears there, I went to Baird Point, a spot by a pond near the dorms where replicas of Roman ruins stood. The symbolism of sitting amidst those ruins was not lost on me. My hopes and dreams for the future, which had once seemed so rock solid and permanent, could be crumbling to dust. I was numb at first, but as the hours and minutes passed, I started to slip into despair and seethe with anger. I did not yet know if the police had caught the people who shot my father and uncle. All I could think of was my seriously wounded father, my weeping mother, and my shocked brothers.

The flight home was a blur. I made it to the hospital and saw many family members in the waiting area. My brothers, my grandparents, my uncles, my cousins, and even family friends, were sitting in stunned silence. When they saw me approaching, they all stood up and came to greet me. My grandmother started to cry right away. My mother tried to stay strong, but as she hugged me, she began to sob. About an hour later, I was permitted to see my father in the intensive care unit. My mother warned me that he was not consistently conscious, that he was moaning in pain, and that he was quite bandaged up.

The room he was in was brightly lit in a way that I can only describe as harsh. There was a lot of noise in the surrounding area as the nurses, interns, and orderlies hurried about taking care of patients. As I entered the room, I was overcome with a strange sense of vertigo when I first saw my father. He was lying still on the bed, his eyes closed. With each breath, he gave out a low, almost inaudible moan. The machines in his room were beeping, pulsating, and flashing. He was dependent on them. He was incapacitated. It was very difficult to behold. I had never before seen my father look helpless or physically weak. Seeing him in that hospital bed was as disorienting as trying to find my way through a pitch-black room.

My father is my hero in many ways. He was physically impressive even though he was not an overly large or muscular man. But I can say without exaggeration that his sheer physical strength was the stuff of legends. As a teenager in Lebanon, he made money by smashing concrete with a sledgehammer and carrying trunks of cedar trees around the mountain village where he was raised. I once saw him tear a window out of a house, along with many of the bricks for the wall, with his bare hands. Countless times he had beaten men twice his size at arm wrestling. He once picked up one end of a Volkswagen and turned it sideways in the street by himself—cutting up his hands in the process—just to prove a point. His strength of body was rivaled only by his strength of heart and courage. Growing up, I thought that my father was as close to a real-life Superman as one could encounter.

But a lowly criminal armed with a .22 caliber pistol tried to take it all away with just the twitch of a finger on a metal trigger. He and his accomplice had no concern for the effect his actions would have on my family. They cared nothing for the man my father was. They gave no thought to the devastation they would bring to so many by cutting my father's and uncle's lives short. The irony was that my father and uncle had worked so hard for so long to build that business, and these men wanted only fast money that they would not have to work for. They wanted it so badly that they were willing to destroy all of our lives for a few hundred dollars.

As I looked on my wounded father in the hospital, I could feel myself begin to change. I could feel the serenity of mind and the easygoing spirit I once had, start to die and be replaced by something ugly. I started to feel an unfamiliar emotion—hate. Certainly I had been angry with and disliked other people before that day, but I had never felt pure hatred before. I had never felt a consuming desire for the downfall of another human being before. In that hospital room, looking at my father in such pain, real hate awoke within me. I truly hated the men who had done this to my father and my family. As I sat back down in the waiting room, I could feel something in me die and something much uglier be born. I embraced the ugly newborn thing inside me. I would not resist it.

Over the ensuing months, my father and my uncle gradually recovered from their wounds, but not without heavy and serious physical costs. The anger and hate in me did not wane, however. To be sure, they ebbed and flowed. But during the times they were less intense, they never fully went away. They were only hibernating. Occasionally, they would awaken and cause me to become very moody and contemplative. I transferred from the University of Buffalo back to the University of Michigan, where I continued my freshman year. But that year, I would walk the downtown Ann Arbor streets in the middle of the night. A part of me hoped that someone would start trouble with me so that I could unleash on that person all the anger I harbored inside. Although I had started that semester with great grades, I barely squeaked by in my classes and even failed one class outright. I was aimless, depressed, and angry.

The police had caught the two men who tried to murder my father and uncle. One of them—the man who had actually pulled the trigger—had copped a plea and agreed to testify against the other at trial. When the trial came, I not only relived all of the shock and anger from that first day in the hospital, but I also experienced true rage. I had finally seen face-to-face the men who had tried to steal our lives away. As I sat in the hallway during a recess in the trial, the man who was to testify against his partner was being brought into the courtroom somewhat near me. I looked at him and began to fantasize about rushing up to him, stealing the gun from the escorting officer, and killing him right there in the hallway. I calmed myself as best I could.

In the courtroom, I sat in the very first row, usually at a distance from my family members. As the defendant testified, I stared holes through him. In an attempt to foster sympathy with the jury, he waxed on about his plans for the future, how he was trying to make something of himself, how his accomplice was really to blame, and how he did not think his life should be ruined by all of this. I could hardly believe my ears. I began to breathe heavily through my nose as I stared at him with utter contempt. To this day, I am not sure if I even blinked during his entire testimony.

During a recess in the testimony, the prosecutor approached

me and asked me to stop staring at the defendant or else leave the courtroom because I was starting to distract the jury. When the testimony resumed, I tried to contain myself. It was nearly impossible, because at that moment my hate overwhelmed my reason. I retreated into my own thoughts. I very seriously entertained the thought of jumping over the attorneys' table and strangling the man with my bear hands until he died in my grip. It was not just a fleeting thought. I actually felt the strong impulse and could feel the muscles in my legs begin to tense up for the jump over the rail that divided the gallery from the witness. Only by sheer force of will was I able to overcome the impulse to exact revenge.

Although he was convicted and sent to prison, I did not feel that justice had been served. I was consumed by sorrow for what I had lost and for what I had almost lost. I felt the need for justice to be satisfied. Was imprisonment justice? Was not death more just? Or would that be revenge? I had to struggle to tell the difference.

In the months and years following that ordeal, I could not help but wonder why God would allow this to happen if He truly loved my family and me. Confused as I was over how God's concern for me could be found in these circumstances, I was not confused about one thing. The men who tried to kill my father and my family's future with him were my sworn enemies. I would never be truly at peace as long as they were breathing. Their acts of violence had transformed me into something I never thought I would become.

Brighter Days

Fast-forward to a much lighter episode in my life about ten years later. Several weeks before our wedding day, my bride-to-be and I sat in the family room of my house, planning the details of the upcoming ceremony. To be completely accurate, we were likely in the third or fourth of our planning sessions. I had always thought I would dread trudging through decisions about color schemes, napkins, invitations, and the like. But for some reason, I was enjoying the experience (as much as men are capable of enjoying such things, anyway). As we sat there that night, we were discussing which portions of Scripture we would want to have read during the ceremony. We had it in our heads that we were going to make things traditional, yet slightly different from the usual wedding ceremony. We had decided right out of the gate that we would not include the ubiquitous thirteenth chapter of 1 Corinthians—the famous "love chapter"—among the Scripture readings, simply because that chapter was always read at weddings and we wanted to do something different. Nicole and I both loved the beautiful words of that famous chapter, but we were set in our desire to be at least a little unconventional. Feeling quite innovative, we decided to have Ruth 1:16–17 and Ephesians 3:14–19 read at our wedding, only to find out later, after attending several weddings, that these passages were not such unique choices after all.

Perhaps it was tradition, perhaps it was force of habit, or perhaps it was the sheer appropriateness of the words, but our pastor decided during the ceremony that he would quote from 1 Corinthians 13. Though I was very much focused on the special quality of the day, I could not help but think, *Is there some kind of rule or doctrine in Protestantism that I'm not aware of that requires 1 Corinthians 13 to be read at weddings?* I decided to enjoy the recitation of the passage and concluded that it is so beautiful that people cannot help but recite it when love is in the air. It seems that to omit 1 Corinthians 13 from a wedding ceremony would be as distracting an omission as going to a sporting event without hearing "The Star-Spangled Banner." It just is not done.

People often hear the words of 1 Corinthians 13, not only at weddings, but also during sermons centering on the themes of human love and interpersonal relationships. The words are so familiar to us that they almost do not need quoting, but the particulars are important.

If I speak with the tongues of men and of angels, but do not have love, I have become a noisy gong or a clanging cymbal. And if I have the gift of prophecy, and know all mysteries and all knowledge; and if I have all faith, so as to remove mountains, but do not have love, I am nothing. And if I give all my possessions to feed the poor, and if I surrender my body to be burned, but do not have love, it profits me nothing. Love is patient, love is kind *and* is not jealous; love does not brag *and* is not arrogant, does not act unbecomingly; it does not seek its own, is not provoked, does not take into account a wrong *suffered,* does not rejoice in unrighteousness, but rejoices with the truth; bears all things, believes all things, hopes all things, endures all things. Love never fails. (1 Cor. 13:1–8a NASB)

The text is quite applicable for wedding ceremonies and sermons about interpersonal relationships, but romantic love was not what Paul was primarily inspired to write about when he penned those famous words.

Several years ago, I had the privilege of listening to one of my favorite Bible teachers give a sermon on 1 Corinthians 13. He pointed out that in describing the many facets of love in the first eight verses, Paul also was describing the attributes of Christ. To illustrate the point, he asked those of us in the audience to mentally substitute "Jesus" in the text wherever the word *love* occurred. He also pointed out that in verses 4 through 8, which begin with the words, "Love is patient," Paul was describing the loving attributes that a Christian should have if he or she truly has been transformed by the power of God and seeks to emulate Christ. To make that point, he asked us to mentally substitute our own name for the word *love* in verses 4 through 8 to see if we were allowing God to transform us into the image of Christ.[2]

I have never forgotten that sermon. It showed me that God is not just in the business of loving us but also in the business of transforming us.

The second part of 1 Corinthians 13 is not always read at weddings, but it actually punctuates the transformative power of the gospel.

> But as for prophecies, they will come to an end; as for languages, they will cease; as for knowledge, it will come to an end. For we know in part, and we prophesy in part. But when the perfect comes, the partial will come to an end. When I was a child, I spoke like a child, I thought like a child, I reasoned like a child. When I became a man, I put aside childish things. For now we see indistinctly, as in a mirror, but then face to face. Now I know in part, but then I will know fully, as I am fully known.
> *Now these three remain: faith, hope, and love. But the greatest of these is love.* (1 Cor. 13:8b–13 HCSB, emphasis added)

There is something important in the last sentence of 1 Corinthians 13. When all gifts, knowledge, and other issues have run their course, when everything has found its fulfillment, three basic things finally remain—faith, hope, and love.

A Tale of Three Things

Faith, hope, and love bear an important relationship to three other things we have explored, namely, the fundamental facets of conflict—sorrow, justice, and love. We have seen how sorrow stems from the loss that comes from conflict. We have seen how the cry for justice rises up from those who have been wronged. We have seen that conflict leads us to ask one of the most important questions anyone can ask: Am I loved? We also have seen that the gospel of Jesus Christ and His crucifixion and resurrection resolve the tensions that exist between these three facets of conflict. The tensions exist because the things at odds with each other lack fulfillment. Resolution is the process by which things in tension with each other are harmonized. Jesus accomplished resolution by experiencing ultimate sorrow through His death on the cross, so that we would not have to. He sacrificed Himself to satisfy divine justice, so that we can have mercy. And He did this because of His infinite, selfless love for us. There is assurance of salvation in the historical reality of what Christ has done for us. We can be confident that when Christ returns, all earthly sorrows will end, all injustices will be righted, and we will commune forever with love incarnate.

But may I suggest that *resolution* of these issues is not the end of the marvelous work of the gospel. There remains something more. That something is *transformation*. In fact, transformation is the prevailing paradigm of the New Testament. Transformation occurs after resolution and goes beyond resolution. Transformation takes something and makes it into something different. But we will see that biblical transformation is not just about changing one thing into another. It is about taking things that have been resolved and changing them into something better, even pure.

God in Christ does not intersect human history merely to solve a problem or cause some event to occur. He does not rescue us from a desperate situation just so that we later fall victim to the same trap. Instead, God transforms a situation, He transforms us, and He transforms our perspectives on life's many questions. When God personally encountered the Old Testament patriarchs, matriarchs, and prophets, He did not leave them as He found them. He changed their names, and He changed their hearts. Abram became Abraham, Sarai became Sarah, and Jacob became Israel. In the New Testament, we see Jesus changing the names of His disciples. Simon He called Peter, and the brothers James and John He called the "sons of thunder." Later, Joses the Cypriot became Barnabas, and Saul of Tarsus became Paul. The message is clear. God is in the business of transformation.

So it is with the three basic and profound facets of conflict.

Sorrow, justice, and love are not just resolved in Christ; they are radically transformed by Him. Sorrow turns into hope, the cry for justice turns into faith, and the desire for love turns into its abiding fulfillment and the way in which we help others now and in the age to come; it is fulfilled in a way that we will love and be loved by one another and God in such a way that we can scarcely comprehend.

Sorrow into Hope

Sorrow is entirely appropriate at times, but, sadly, most people's sorrow is without hope (cf. 1 Thess. 4:13). A parent clutching the lifeless body of a child killed by a bomb or a land mine no longer has any hope for that child's future in this world. That child will not grow up. He will not learn new things, he will not make mistakes, and he will not meet the girl of his dreams and marry her. There is nothing of expectation left for his future. It has been cut off prematurely by the rage and sin that fuels conflict. In this sense, then, we can see that such sorrow is the very opposite of hope, just as it is the very opposite of joy. Hope is the expectation of something good and pure to happen in the future. It is the patient waiting for something better than the present circumstances. It looks toward the future. If sorrow brings hopelessness, then the resolution of sorrow through the Cross is indeed profound and necessary to fulfill the purpose of human existence. But it is not enough. There must be a transformation of sorrow into its very opposite, which is hope. Once again, the cross of Christ offers that transformation. More to the point, Jesus' resurrection offers us the hope for something redeeming in our future. Jesus' resurrection demonstrates His power over death and validates His promise that He will make all things new and that, when He does so, there will be no more death and thus no despair. Indeed, the gospel message is that in the future for the believer in Christ, "there will no longer be any mourning, or crying, or pain; the first things have passed away" (Rev. 21:4 NASB).

That hope is not just a future "pie-in-the-sky" sentiment. The reality of Jesus' resurrection allows those who grieve now for lost loved ones to carry on as their sorrow is turned to hope. So for those parents who lost children in the village of Qana when it was bombed in 2006 and for those Jews who have lost loved ones from suicide bombings in the public square, there can be a transformation that provides strength to endure amid conflict.

Justice to Faith

Closely related to hope, but certainly distinct from it, is faith. Jesus transforms the cry for justice into faith. The cry for justice comes when an injustice has been worked on us. We cry out for justice and even demand it in protests and vigils, because injustice is the opposite of our expectations. We expect others to treat us justly. But as we have already seen, we do not always desire justice in response to our own actions. Rather, we want mercy from others. But that does not make the desire for justice illegitimate. That desire for justice is an inherent quality written on our hearts because we are made in God's image. But injustice is not merely a disappointment of our expectations. It is an assault on our trust in a system of balance that is fundamental to our existence. When we submit ourselves to a system of justice, we do so, trusting that justice indeed will result from that system. But when the system breaks down, when the innocent are punished and the guilty go scot-free, our trust is betrayed. Where once we were confident in a justice system, our confidence is shattered. Thus, injustice is not just unfairness; it is the very murder of our trust.

Faith, then, is the opposite of injustice. Faith, especially as used in the Bible, is defined as a confident trust in something or someone. Faith is not just a trust that something probably will happen or that someone probably will deliver on a promise. It is a confident trust that what is promised is inevitable.

In fact, faith is used almost exclusively in the Bible as trust in someone, specifically God and Christ. It is a trust that God is capable of doing what He promised. It is a trust that He will provide deliverance. The writer of the letter to the Hebrews provides a very interesting definition of faith. "Faith," he writes, "is the substance of things hoped for, the evidence of things not seen" (Heb. 11:1 KJV). The relationship between faith and hope is made explicit in this verse, as faith is the *substance* of things hoped for. This means that faith is actually more than hope because it is more substantial. Hope is an expectation for something positive and good; faith is more than just an expectation. Faith is a trust, a confidence that something *will* happen, despite indications to the contrary.

Biblically speaking, faith is not trust in abstract ideas or mindless concepts. We speak in common parlance of having "faith in the justice system" or "faith in the goodness of humanity." But the Bible rarely, if ever, speaks of someone having faith in systems or abstract ideas. When the Bible describes faith, it is in the context of one's faith in *someone*, namely, God. The Old Testament actually has no word only for faith as the Greek New Testament does. In the Old Testament, the Hebrew word translated "faith" actually means "faithfulness," which is the quality of having trust in God because His consistency and proven power make Him trustworthy. In the letter to the Hebrews, the writer defines faith as having another concrete facet. It is "the evidence of things not seen." This may seem like a strange phrase to us today because we have come to think of faith as a belief in something despite a lack of evidence for it. In some contexts, that can be the meaning. But in most biblical contexts, faith or faithfulness is itself the evidence of God's trustworthiness. Abraham trusted that, despite his wife's barrenness and his own advanced years, God would grant him children who would multiply into many nations (Gen. 17:5). His trust did not come from wishful thinking but rather because he heard this promise from God firsthand and had witnessed God's work in other ways. We see that example carried throughout the Bible. The writer of Hebrews follows up his statement that faith is the evidence of things not seen by listing the faithful acts of many in the Old Testament. What he is communicating is that those acts of faith, in and of themselves, are evidence of things not seen. Faith is an affirmative act of trust based on a valid reason to offer that trust.

But what about us? Most of us have never witnessed an irrefutable miracle and we have not heard God's voice in an audible sense. And what about those who cling to other faiths? Can their faithfulness also be "evidence of things not seen?" Faith is only as valid as its object. One can have faith in a statue in the living room, but that faith will prove to be quite worthless when the trust in that object is finally put to the test. One can have faith in a system or a method or a path that seems to work in this world, but when we are called to account and are face-to-face with God, will the path or plan we have trusted in let us down? The question we have to answer is, should such confident trust be placed in Jesus? The answer is yes, because, like the prophets and disciples of old, we too have strong evidence upon which to base our faith.

Jesus' resurrection from the dead is not a flight of fancy cooked up by a cadre of frightened fisherman and tax collectors. As we look through the annals of history as recounted by both Christians and non-Christians alike, we can see the solid evidence for the historicity of the resurrection. That evidence is rich with detail and established even by the testimony of the enemies of Christianity. The resurrection of Christ is as well established as any other fact of history. Its probability is something we can place our trust in. And if it is something worthy of our trust, then it follows that we can have a confident trust in the promises that came from the lips of the one who prophesied that He would die and rise again. He promised to rule with justice and to reward each according to what he or she has done. At the cross, Jesus took on our punishment so that justice could be served. But in His resurrection, the cry of injustice is not just resolved but transformed. It is transformed into faith—a confident trust and expectation that the one who can raise Himself from the dead can, indeed, make all things right.

Inward Love to Outward Love

The questions about love that arise from conflict are directed inward. Because of conflict, we experience sorrow and injustice and look with futility to an indifferent world, only to be left to wonder whether we are loved by the outside world and even whether God loves us. Once we realize that God does love us, and loved us to such an extent that Jesus went to the cross, then the tension between our inward need for love and its seeming lack of fulfillment is resolved.

God has shown His infinite love for us by paying an infinite price so that we can share with Him in the infinity to come. By definition, the infinite quality of that love is more than enough to fill anyone's individual longing for love. While we rightly look for healthy and loving relationships in this life even after having experienced the infinite love that God offers, we do not do so because our souls are still lonely and unfulfilled. Once Christ dwells in the temple of the human heart, our search for earthly relationships is not driven by a need to satiate a lonely thirst for love. We look for relationships because God has instilled the desire for relationships within us.

When our hearts have been filled beyond measure, our focus on love is transformed. We no longer need to ask ourselves, *Am I loved? Does God love me?* The answers have been dramatically and conclusively given. Thus, our very questions are transformed. When we look at another person, especially one caught in the desperate search for love, we now ask ourselves, *Does that person know that the infinite God infinitely loves him or her? What can I do for that person that will reflect the love of the Jesus I know?* We seek to offer people Christ by offering them Christlike love as we extend the unconditional kindnesses that Christ extended to us. Perhaps that is why in 1 Corinthians 13:13, Paul refers to love as the "greatest of these" things that remain. Hope can be shared, and it is inwardly beneficial. The same holds true for faith. When love is shared with others, it gives them hope and bolsters their faith. The "greatest of these is love," not because it is a more intense emotion, but because "God is love" (1 John 4:8); and love in its eternality is not to be hoarded but shared and expressed for the benefit of others.

Transformation That Leads to Action

These transformations are not just passive changes in our outlook with no action on our part. There can be no idleness in hope, faith, or love. We do not sit around hoping for something better. We do not inactively wait in faith for God to accomplish what He has promised. We do not wallow in a sense of self-centered love that affects only us. When our sorrows, demands for justice, and desire for love are resolved and transformed, we become more sensitive to others' cries of sorrow, demands for justice, and need for love. This new sensitivity should stir believers in Christ to action that positively impacts the world around us and points the world to Christ and His cross.

It is no accident that in 1 Thessalonians, to one of the earliest of his letters, Paul alludes to the active nature of faith, hope, and love. He commends the Thessalonians for being instrumental in the spread of the gospel of peace throughout their area. Specifically, Paul writes that the gospel is advanced because of the Thessalonians' "work produced by faith," their "labor prompted by love," and their "endurance inspired by hope" (1 Thess. 1:3 NIV). For Paul, faith, love, and hope are not just nouns. They are verbs. They are words of action.

To highlight this, Paul provides an active metaphor for faith, hope, and love in the same letter to the Thessalonians. He writes in chapter 5 that the believer in Christ is to stand as a beacon of light amidst darkness, in a warrior's stance. "But since we are of the day, we must be sober and put the armor of faith and love on our chests, and put on a helmet of the hope of salvation" (1 Thess. 5:8 HCSB). This warrior imagery provides us with a poetic and powerful paradox. Conflict results in the tensions between sorrow, justice, and love. Yet Paul uses battle armor to illustrate the power of the transformation of these facets into faith, hope, and love. The armor of faith, hope, and love keeps our spirits safe and expectant for the future during conflict and upheaval. In fact, in 1 Thessalonians 5, Paul is encouraging the Thessalonians to be steadfast in their faith, hope, and love during significant troubles to come. Paul teaches us not to keep a distance from the bloody battles all around us but to march into the breach, protected by faith, hope, and love. We are to wear these pieces of armor not to fight for land, power, or wealth, but to wage true peace and offer it to the hearts of those for whom conflict and suffering are the chief characteristics of life.

Some have observed a passivity in the spiritual life that looks to the future. In discussing Jewish religious hope for the future, Gershom Scholem observes,

> There is something grand about living in hope, but at the same time there is something profoundly unreal about it. It diminishes the singular worth of the individual, and he can never fulfill himself, because the incompleteness of his endeavors eliminates precisely what constitutes its highest value. Thus in Judaism the Messianic idea has compelled *a life lived in deferment*, in which nothing can be done definitively, nothing can be irrevocably accomplished. . . . Precisely understood, there is nothing concrete which can be accomplished by the unredeemed. This makes for the greatness of Messianism, but also for its constitutional weakness.[3]

Scholem's comment is insightful in some respects, but it holds true only if one's hope is either misplaced or unfulfilled. With respect to messianic hopes, Scholem's observation is valid only if Messiah has not yet come in His first advent and if Jesus is not that Messiah.

But Messiah has come and will come again, and Jesus is Messiah. As I have already stated, history tells us that Jesus rose from the dead in confirmation of his claim to be Messiah. In fact, Jesus' death and resurrection were not just confirmations of his messiahship; they were also integral and necessary to it. The Messiah is the one who is to bring peace. Many Jews today, like millions of Jews since the first century, look for someone other than Jesus as the coming Messiah. They continue to look for another because they believe that when Messiah comes, He will bring world peace by bringing an end to world conflict. Because Jesus did not bring such peace, He must not be Messiah. But as we have seen, true peace is not merely the absence of conflict. It is the quietness of the soul—the *shalom, salaam,* and *eirene*—that comes when the spiritual issues emanating from conflict are resolved and transformed.

Jesus brought and still offers us that true peace. He Himself is our peace. Thus, for the follower of Christ, there is no "living in deferment" for the hope of that deliverance and redemption. It already has occurred. Contrary to Scholem's observations, the hopeful and faithful believers in Jesus can achieve concrete accomplishments here and now because they *are* redeemed. The most concrete accomplishment is the sharing of the peace that Jesus embodies with others so that they too can have that same assurance vouchsafed and made secure by Jesus' sacrifice and historical resurrection. For each person who prostrates himself before the Lord and realizes that he is not saved because he is special or better than others, but saved despite his lack of specialness and his lack of merit, there is another person who sees that his enemies are not people lower than himself. In fact, he sees that his enemies are not actually people. His enemies are despair, unbelief, and hate, which so easily find nests in the heart of humanity. In this way, conflict itself becomes transformed when we embrace the gospel.

Conflict is no longer about people to fight against but about souls to fight for.

While it is true that nothing can be concretely accomplished by the unredeemed, in Christ we can be and are redeemed. If messianism's constitutional weakness is that life is lived in deferment because we remain unredeemed, then there is good news for all. Our lives are no longer in deferment. We no longer need to wait for the Messiah and the peace He brings to each of us. He has come, and His peace has come.

Some have called this faith in what has happened before and the hope for what will happen in the future as the "already/not yet" facet of Christian theology and the Christian life. Jesus has "already" come and given us peace, but the establishment of the new creation is "not yet." We stand in faith on what God has done at the cross and the empty tomb, but we wait for the future time when God will cut off the "bow of war" and peace will reign from the Euphrates to the end of the earth (Zech. 9:10). But we do not live in deferment to some future date. We live consistently with our confident trust that the God who raised Jesus from the dead also can bring about the new creation He promised. That is faith. We live in expectation of that which is not yet—Christ's second coming, when death will be no more and sorrow shall end. That is hope. And we act toward others, even those who would draw racial or geographical boundaries and call themselves our enemies, as Christ has acted toward us—with compassion and selflessness. That is love.

The Second Transformation

In the years that followed my father's shooting, I began an intense investigation into the validity of the various world-views we are all offered. The shooting is not what prompted that search. Indeed, my investigation had already begun to some extent by then. What fueled my search was an internal challenge. I determined that I would not give my allegiance to a worldview just because I was born into that worldview.

Rather, I would investigate the theistic, nontheistic, and even atheistic worldviews and place my trust in the one that is backed by sound reasoning and evidence. During my journey, while still a Muslim but looking at the gospel with an open mind, I read a statement by the apostle Paul that alludes to the gospel being the means by which enemies in conflict can be at peace because sorrow, justice, and love are transformed into hope, faith, and selfless love.

> Therefore, having been justified by *faith*, we have peace with God through our Lord Jesus Christ, through whom also we have obtained our introduction by *faith* into this grace in which we stand; and we exult in *hope* of the glory of God. And not only this, but we also exult in our *tribulations*, knowing that tribulation brings about perseverance; and perseverance, proven character; and proven character, *hope*; and *hope* does not disappoint, because the *love* of God has been poured out within our hearts through the Holy Spirit who was given to us. (Rom. 5:1–5 NASB, emphases mine)

These words struck me as quite powerful. But as I read the next verses, I was truly undone.

> For while we were still helpless, at the right time Christ died for the ungodly. For one will hardly die for a righteous man; though perhaps for the good man someone would dare even to die. *But God demonstrates His own love toward us, in that while we were yet sinners, Christ died for us.* (Rom. 5:6–8 NASB, emphasis added)

I read and reread those verses for days and even weeks. During that time, it became quite clear to me that there is no message offered to us like the gospel message. Paul says quite bluntly that in our rebellious nature, we are at enmity with God. No, it is actually worse—we have made God our enemy.

What is unique in this message is that God does not exact retribution on us for making Him our enemy, though He has every moral right to do so, but does just the opposite. God demonstrates to us that He loves us in that while we were yet His enemies—while we hated God—God incarnate in the person of Jesus died to save us from the damnation that follows our own hate.

This truth had such a powerful impact on me because when I had first read Romans 5, I was steeped in hate for the men who had tried to destroy my family's life. Though years had passed since that awful incident, not a week had gone by that I did not find myself in contemplative anger over what had happened. I did not want mercy for those criminals. I wanted revenge. But as I let Romans 5 sink in, I came to realize who Christ is and who I was in comparison. During the trial, I had fantasized about choking the very life out of the men who had tried to kill my father and uncle. I had even fantasized that someone would burst into the courtroom during the trial and shoot them both dead. Not only did I truly hate those men, but I could not even fathom being capable of having the slightest concern for them. In no way did I commit any violence against either man. But the lack of violence did not change the fact that I was neck deep in conflict over what they had done to us. Despite a lack of violence since that day, I was impossibly far from having any peace.

Through the lens of Romans 5, I finally was able to see the depth and breadth of God's character in Christ. To be frank, I saw in God the exact opposite of myself. God sacrificed, not to save His friends or those who loved Him, but to save His enemies. That is exactly what Paul means when he says that Christ died for the ungodly and for sinners. I suddenly realized that if Jesus were in my place and someone had burst into that courtroom to shoot the men who had tried to kill someone He loved, Jesus would not have sat by and smiled with approval. *He would have jumped out of His seat and taken the bullet Himself.* He would have given His life to save His enemy.

Christ would do what I could not even fathom doing myself. With this realization, my conflicted mind and heart were sent reeling.

What kind of love is this?

This kind of love is wholly different from any human love I have ever known.

This kind of love is so pure that it cannot be the love of a mere man.

Jesus tells us that we should love our enemies and pray for those who persecute us (Matt. 5:44). Many people have said such things in an effort to give their worldviews appeal, as a corollary to their belief that "all you need is love." But Jesus, at the Place of the Skull, was the only founder of a worldview who gave actual teeth to the phrase "love your enemies." He is the only one who walked the talk, as it were. He told us to love our enemies, and at the Cross He did just that.

When Jesus was crucified, two criminals also were crucified alongside Him, one on His right and another on His left. As some in the crowd began to hurl insults at Him, the two criminals joined in (Matt. 27:44). Later, however, as they hung there slowly dying, one of the criminals had a change of heart. Perhaps he looked on Jesus' immeasurable suffering and was moved within himself. As the other criminal again began to mock Jesus, the penitent criminal rebuked him. Changed by the power of Jesus' crucifixion, he found faith in Jesus and pleaded, "Jesus, remember me when You come into Your kingdom!" (Luke 23:42 NASB). With love for this man, this criminal who was His enemy, Jesus promised him eternal life: "I assure you: Today you will be with Me in paradise" (Luke 23:43 HCSB).

Jesus embodies what it means to truly love one's enemies. Jesus loved the criminal dying next to Him, who was once His enemy. Jesus cared for the Samaritan woman at Jacob's well— although the Samaritans were enemies of the Jews. In Romans 5, Paul recognized the profundity of Jesus' act at the Cross.

Reading the words in Romans 5, two impossibly dramatic things happened to me at the same time. First, I finally saw who God truly is. I saw divine love personified in Jesus. Second, I finally saw that to fully understand the gospel and to understand who I was before God, I had to put myself in the place of the men who had tried to rob and murder my father and uncle. Though I had not tried to rob someone or take another person's life like they had, darkness lurked in my own heart. For years I could not even conceive of having compassion for those men. Now I realized that God has done for me what I could not imagine doing for anyone else. I had been consumed by my own sorrow, my own demand for justice, and my doubts about the depth of God's love. As Paul's words in Romans 5 sank into my soul, I pictured Jesus, torn and tattered, bruised and battered, hanging on the cross. I pictured Him looking out at the crowd gathered around Him.

Some followed Him; some hated Him.

He died for them all.

He died for me, though I was His enemy.

On that cross, Jesus accomplished two impossibly dramatic things at the same time. He resolved my sorrow, my cry for justice, and my doubts about His love. And in accomplishing that resolution, He also transformed my heart. He transformed my sorrow into hope, my longing for justice into faith, and my desire to be loved into a desire to share the love of Christ with others, even my enemies.

The transformative power referenced in 1 Corinthians 13, which results from Jesus' work on the cross, is the agent for real change in the world. For every person who truly embraces the kind of love for our enemies that Christ embodies, there will be one less person consumed with the kind of conflict-driven bitterness that causes a person to strap a bomb to his or her chest or to view someone of another ethnicity with contempt.

The former prime minister of Israel Golda Meir once said that there will be peace between Jews and Arabs when the Arabs "love their children more than they hate us." Respectfully, I beg to differ. First, this kind of statement assumes that only one side of the conflict is steeped in hate. That just does not reflect the reality of human nature, especially during war. Second, and more fundamentally, the Middle East Conflict will stop only when all sides start seeing who they are before God and who God is by looking at the remarkable Cross. The gospel tells us that, fundamentally, we are not enemies of each other; rather, we have made ourselves enemies of God. Both our inward and outward perspectives must be transformed. Our hate must be transformed. And only God can accomplish that level of transformation. Peace does not come when "they" have been defeated. Peace comes when we love our enemies as Christ loved His enemies. He loved them, not by seeking their destruction, but by seeking their redemption.

Is there any concrete example we can look to for hope that the age-old combatants in the Middle East can find peace among themselves through Christ? Interestingly, a potent example comes to us from the true story of World War I's "Christmas Truce."

In the winter of 1914, the First World War was only five months old. In that short time, approximately 800,000 men had been wounded or killed. On France's Western Front, British and German soldiers had been fiercely fighting. On Christmas Eve in 1914, the soldiers braced themselves for another day of blood and bombs. But things would be different from the previous days.

British soldiers in the trenches had spontaneously raised signs bearing the message "Merry Christmas" and began singing Christmas carols. Soon, the British soldiers could hear Christmas carols coming from the German trenches. On Christmas morning, both the German and British soldiers left their trenches, even though officers on both sides unsuccessfully tried to stop them. The soldiers met in the middle of no-man's land and sang songs and engaged in conversations. They exchanged sweets and cigars and in one spot, the British and the Germans played soccer together. In some places along the front, the spontaneous truce continued into the next day, with neither side willing to fire the first shot. But the truce ended when fresh troops arrived and the commanders of both armies ordered that any similar conduct would be punishable as treason.[4]

Fierce enemies, who only days before had been engaged in fierce combat, had acted as if they were brothers. The profundity of the event is found not just in the fact that the two sides had ceased fighting but also in the fact that they embraced one another and for a sweet but short time had community. They did so because the story of the birth of the Prince of Peace had entered their hearts. If it was possible then, amid the horrors of the World War I trenches, it is possible anywhere, even in the Middle East.

For years my heart was immersed in conflict over what two criminals did to my family. But now I have peace despite that conflict because Jesus transformed my sorrow, cry for justice, and doubts about love into hope, faith, and surety about love. I once thought I would do unspeakable things to those men if I could be alone with either of them in a locked room without windows. I now believe that if I could see those men alone, I would speak to them about the lengths to which God went to offer them redemption.

I close this book just as I began it—discussing eschatology and what is to come. We began by examining whether Christians are focusing too heavily on debating the details of the end times and how that debate has negatively impacted our efforts to spread the primary message of the gospel—that Jesus and Jesus alone provides the resolution of life's most pressing issues, which are in tension with each other and with our very souls. Though we have come full circle and must recognize that the end times are vitally important to think about, we still have to consider the question I first posed in chapter 1, which derived from C. S. Lewis's observation that God shouts to us in the midst of suffering and conflict. The question is this: If you are a follower of Christ who is commanded to shout God's message to this world, what message will you shout to a lost and dying world that suffers amid conflict?

Will you shout your eschatological views, proclaiming who should have entitlements based on the privilege of heritage or DNA, and thus alienate the opposing side in the process?

Or will you shout the gospel of Jesus Christ—that at the Cross and empty tomb, there is resolution and transformation of every issue that arises from conflict?

Will you shout at all?

Jesus commanded His followers to shout and to shout the gospel. For the Christian, is there really any alternative that still allows us to keep our integrity? Can followers of Christ honestly reflect on the agony Jesus underwent for their sins and the sins of the world and yet keep the news of His redeeming work a secret, especially when conflict presents us with such profound opportunities to shout about what it means to have true peace? The opportunities to shout are not just overseas in war-torn countries, but also right across the fence to your neighbors' yard, right across the cubicle partition in your office, and wherever you find yourself.

Allow me to close with a final quote. It is a quote from the most famous hymn ever written. "Amazing Grace" was written by John Newton, who was transformed from the captain of a slave ship to a champion for the abolition of slavery after He encountered Christ. An unknown author wrote the last stanza, which so beautifully touches on the future glory and peace we confidently wait for with faith, hope, and love.

> When we've been there ten thousand years,
> Bright shining as the sun,
> We've no less days to sing God's praise
> Than when we'd first begun.

If you are a believer in Christ, you are basking in the anticipation of that time of peace. But you also know that nonbelieving Jews, Muslims, and others all around us will not have the blissful peace of that time, nor the present peace that comes from knowing that such an eternity awaits, unless they embrace the gospel truth.

True peace is missing throughout this world, not just in the war-weary regions of the Middle East. The missing piece of the peace we are missing is not a political strategy, a treaty, or an accord. The missing piece is not the universal acceptance of a well-argued eschatological view. The missing piece of the missing peace is a person—Jesus Christ, who "Himself is our peace."

BIBLIOGRAPHY

Accad, Martin, "Another Point of View: Evangelical Blindness on Lebanon." Christianity Today, http://www.christianity today.com/ct/2006/julyweb-only/129-42.0.html.

Andrew, Brother, and Al Janseen. *Light Force: A Stirring Account of the Church Caught in the Middle East Crossfire.* Grand Rapids: Revell, 2004.

Barbet, P. *A Doctor at Calvary: The Passion of Our Lord Jesus Christ as Described by a Surgeon.* Garden City, NY: Doubleday, 1953.

Brickner, David. "Mixing Politics and Religion." http://www .jewsforjesus.org/publications/realtime/52/01.

Burge, Gary M. *Whose Land? Whose Promise? What Christians Are Not Being Told About Israel and the Palestinians.* Cleveland: Pilgrim, 2003.

Carter, Jimmy. *Palestine Peace Not Apartheid.* New York: Simon & Schuster, 2007.

Chesterton, G. K. *Orthodoxy.* New York: Doubleday, 2001.

———. *What's Wrong with the World.* San Francisco: Ignatius Press, 1994.

Cragg, Kenneth. *Jesus and the Muslim.* Oxford: Oneworld Publications, 1999.

Dale, R. W. *The Atonement.* London: Congregational Union of England and Wales, 1894.

Diprose, Ronald E. *Israel and the Church: The Origin and Effects of Replacement Theology*. Waynesboro, GA: Authentic Media, 2004.

Edwards, William D., Wesley J. Gabel, and Floyd E. Hosmer, "On the Physical Death of Jesus." *Journal of the American Medical Association* 255, no. 11 (March 21, 1986): 1456.

Evans, Michael D. *The American Prophecies: Ancient Scriptures Reveal Our Nation's Future*. New York: Warner Faith, 2004.

Fisk, Robert. *Pity the Nation: The Abduction of Lebanon*. 4th ed. New York: Thunder's Mouth Press, 2002.

Foxe, John. *Foxe's Book of Martyrs: A History of the Lives, Sufferings, and Deaths of the Early Christian and Protestant Martyrs*, edited by William Byron Forbush. Grand Rapids: Zondervan, 1967.

Fruchtenbaum, Arnold G. "The Little Apocalypse of Zechariah." In *The End Times Controversy*, edited by Tim LaHaye and Thomas Ice. Eugene, OR: Harvest House, 2003.

Gaebelin, Arno C. *The Conflict of the Ages: The Mystery of Lawlessness, Its Origin, Historic Development, and Coming Defeat*. Vienna, VA: The Exhorters, n.d.

Geisler, Norman L. "Review of Hank Haneraaff's *The Apocalypse Code*." http://www.preteristarchive.com/Critical Articles/geisler-norman_07_01.html.

Glasser, Arthur F. "Eschatology and Christianity's Future in the Middle East." *Missionary Monthly*, April–May 1996, 11.

Habermas, Gary R. *The Risen Jesus and Future Hope*. Lanham, MD: Rowman and Littlefield, 1996.

Habermas, Gary R., and Michael R. Licona. *The Case for the Resurrection of Jesus*. Grand Rapids: Kregel, 2004.

Hanegraaff, Hank. *The Apocalypse Code*. Nashville: Nelson, 2007.

Hanser, Martin H. *The Westminster Collection of Christian Quotations*. Louisville: Westminster/John Knox Press, 2001.

The Humanist Manifesto III, http://www.americanhumanist .org/3/HumanismanditsAspirations.pdf.

Jeremias, Joachim. *The Central Message of the New Testament*. Philadelphia: Fortress, 1965.

Johnson, Phillip E. *Darwin on Trial*. 2nd ed. Downers Grove, IL: InterVarsity Press, 1993.

Kaiser, Walter C., Jr., Peter H. Davids, F. F. Bruce, and Manfred T. Brauch. *The Hard Sayings of the Bible*. 4th ed. Downers Grove, IL: InterVarsity Press, 1996.

Keener, Craig S. *IVP Bible Background Commentary*: New Testament. 2nd ed. Downers Grove, IL: InterVarsity Press, 1994.

LaHaye, Tim, and Jerry B. Jenkins. *Left Behind* Series. 16 vols. Wheaton, IL: Tyndale House, 2000.

Lewis, C. S. *Christian Reflections*. Grand Rapids: Eerdmans, 1967.

———. *Mere Christianity*. New York: Macmillan, 1952.

———. *The Problem of Pain*. New York: HarperCollins, 1996.

Licona, Michael R. *Paul Meets Muhammad: A Christian-Muslim Debate on the Resurrection*. Grand Rapids: Baker, 2006.

Lindsey, Hal. *Apocalypse Code*. Palos Verdes, CA: Western Front, 1997.

———. *The Late Great Planet Earth*, Grand Rapids: Zondervan, 1970.

Loden, Lisa. "Differing Eschatological Viewpoints: Obstacles to Relationship?" *Mishkan* 35, 2001.

Maalouf, Tony. *Arabs in the Shadow of Israel: The Unfolding of God's Prophetic Plan for Ishmael's Line*. Grand Rapids: Kregel, 2003.

Merkley, Paul Charles. *Christian Attitudes Towards the State of Israel*. Montreal: McGill-Queen's University Press, 2001.

Miss Congeniality. DVD, directed by Donald Petrie. Burbank, CA: Warner Home Video, 2004.

Moaz, Baruch. *Priorities in Eschatology*. Rishon L'Tzion: Hagefen, 1991.

Morris, Leon. *The Atonement: Its Meaning and Significance*. Downers Grove, IL: InterVarsity Press, 1983.

Morris, Thomas V. *The Logic of God Incarnate*. Eugene, OR: Wipf and Stock, 2001.

Moyers, Bill. *Bill Moyers' Journal.* http://www.pbs.org/moyers/journal/10052007/transcript2.html.

Munayer, Salim J., ed. *Seeking and Pursuing Peace: The Process, the Pain, and the Product.* Jerusalem: Musalaha, 1998.

Murray, Abdu. "Jesus, Justification, and Justice." http://www.4truth.net/site/c.hiKXLbPNLrF/b.2904181/k.D415/Jesus_Just-fication_and_Justice_Answering_Objections_to_the_Justness_of_Jesus_Sub-stitutionary_Atonement_Apologetics.htm.

Neusner, Jacob, William S. Green, and Ernest S. Frerichs, eds. *Judaisms and Their Messiahs at the Turn of the Christian Era.* New York: Cambridge University Press, 1987.

Oehser, John. "Spreading His Message." http://www.colts.com/sub.dfm?page=article7&news_id=5112730f-a6be-4130-a27d-0d464cd7808d.

Patai, Raphael. *The Messiah Texts.* New York: Avon Books, 1979.

Perrin, Norman. *Rediscovering the Teaching of Jesus.* New York: Harper and Row, 1967.

Reiter, Richard R., Pauld D. Feinberg, Gleason L. Archer Jr., and Douglas J. Moo. *Three Views on the Rapture.* Grand Rapids: Zondervan, 1984.

Said, Edward W. *The End of the Peace Process: Oslo and After.* New York: First Vintage Books, 2001.

Stott, John R. W. *The Cross of Christ: 20th Anniversary Edition.* Downers Grove, IL: InterVarsity Press, 2006.

Strong, James. *The Strongest Strong's Exhaustive Concordance of the Bible.* Fully revised and corrected by John R. Kohlenberger and James A Swanson. Grand Rapids: Zondervan, 2001.

Warraq, Abu 'Isa al-. *Against the Trinity: Anti-Christian Polemic in Early Islam.* Edited and translated by David Thomas. Cambridge: Cambridge University Press, 1992.

Weintraub, Stanley. *Silent Night: The Story of the World War I Christmas Truce.* New York: Free Press, 2001.

Yancey, Philip. *Soul Survivor: How Thirteen Unlikely Mentors Helped My Faith Survive the Church.* New York: Doubleday, 2001.

Zacharias, Ravi K. *Can Man Live Without God.* New York: W
  Publishing Group, 1994.
————. *Jesus Among Other Gods: The Absolute Claims of the
  Christian Message.* Nashville: W Publishing Group, 2000.

NOTES

Chapter 1: Sorrow, Justice, and Love

1. In the twentieth century and into the twenty-first, the eschatological facets of dispensationalism have gained widespread popularity through Hal Lindsey's nonfiction books, *The Late Great Planet Earth* (Grand Rapids: Zondervan, 1970), and *Apocalypse Code* (Palos Verdes, CA: Western Front, 1997). More recently, the best-selling *Left Behind* series (Wheaton, IL: Tyndale House) of fiction books by Tim LaHaye and Jerry B. Jenkins has carried the torch for dispensationalism's popularity.

2. Martin Accad, "Another Point of View: Evangelical Blindness on Lebanon," Christianity Today, http://www.christianitytoday.com/ct/2006/julyweb-only/129-42.0.html (accessed July 20, 2006). Reprinted with author's permission.

3. C. S. Lewis, *The Problem of Pain* (New York: HarperCollins, 1996), 91.

4. John Oehser, "Spreading His Message," http://www.colts.com/sub.dfm?page=article7&news_id=5112730f-a6be-4130-a27d-0d464cd7808d, February 4, 2006 (accessed March 7, 2007).

5. Ibid.

6. Ibid.

Chapter 2: Stumbling Blocks

1. Michael D. Evans, *The American Prophecies: Ancient Scriptures Reveal Our Nation's Future* (New York: Warner Faith, 2004), 193.

2. Arno C. Gaebelein, *The Conflict of the Ages: The Mystery of Lawlessness, Its Origin, Historic Development, and Coming Defeat,* uncensored reprint ed. (Vienna, VA: The Exhorters, n.d.), 147.

3. David Brickner, "Mixing Politics and Religion," http://www.jewsforjesus.org/publications/realtime/52/01 (accessed October 16, 2007).

4. Ibid., citing *Bill Moyers' Journal,* http://www.pbs.org/moyers/journal/10052007/transcript2.html? (accessed October 16, 2007).

5. John R. W. Stott, *The Cross of Christ: 20th Anniversary Edition* (Downers Grove, IL: InterVarsity Press, 2006), 334 (emphasis in original).

6. G. K. Chesterton, *What's Wrong with the World* (San Francisco: Ignatius Press, 1994), 37.

7. Paul's words were not intended to be limited literally to those whose ethnicity is Greek or Jewish. Paul's use of the word *Greek* is a common reference to non-Jews, or Gentiles. Thus, many consider the terms "Greek" and "Gentile" to be interchangeable in Paul's writings.

8. It could be argued that Paul was addressing Christians and that attempting to apply Paul's words here to illustrate how the church should communicate with unbelievers is a stretch. Indeed, Paul was addressing a body of believers, but that body was young, inexperienced in terms of the gospel, and in serious danger of forsaking the essential importance of that gospel. In this way, the Corinthian church quite closely resembles today's nominal Christians or perhaps even non-Christians. In fact, Paul stresses the message he "first" delivered to them, when they were not yet Christians. Thus, I think this passage is particularly applicable.

9. Gary R. Habermas and Michael R. Licona, *The Case for the Resurrection of Jesus* (Grand Rapids: Kregel, 2004), 259–60nn. 24–25.

10. Ibid.

11. Walter C. Kaiser Jr., Peter H. Davids, F. F. Bruce, and Manfred T. Brauch, *The Hard Sayings of the Bible,* 4th ed. (Downers Grove, IL: InterVarsity Press, 1996), 427.

12. Arnold G. Fruchtenbaum, "The Little Apocalypse of Zechariah," in *The End Times Controversy*, ed. Tim LaHaye and Thomas Ice (Eugene, OR: Harvest House, 2003), 262.

13. This number is my calculation based on population and death rate data available from the Central Intelligence Agency's 2008 The World Factbook, available online at www.cia.gov/library/publications/the-world-factbook/index.html.

14. As an example of well-respected Christian leaders holding to different positions, see Hank Hanegraaff's book, *The Apocalypse Code* (Nashville: Thomas Nelson, 2007), which criticizes dispensational eschatology and its geopolitical outworking. For an equally compelling response to Hanegraaff's work, see Norman L. Geisler's "Review of Hank Haneraaff's *The Apocalypse Code*," http://www.preterist archive.com/CriticalArticles/geisler-norman_07-01.html (accessed September 2, 2007). It should be noted that Hanegraaff and Geisler are good friends and are in agreement on the essentials of Christian doctrine. In my opinion, both do an excellent job of making their respective cases.

15. Richard R. Reiter, "A History of the Development of the Raption Positions," in *Three Views on the Rapture*, by Richard R. Reiter, Paul D. Feinberg, Gleason L. Archer Jr., and Douglas J. Moo (Grand Rapids: Zondervan, 1984), 26, citing Robert Cameron, "Notes by the Way," *Watchword and Truth* 35 (December 1913): 377.

16. Raphael Patai, *The Messiah Texts* (New York: Avon Books, 1979), 107, 166.

17. Ibid. The apocryphal writing 4 Ezra 7:27–30, dated several centuries after the writing of the book of Daniel, also depicts a suffering Messiah. In later Talmudic writings, the idea that the Messiah would be slain was further propagated. See B. Suka 52a.

18. See Patai, *The Messiah Texts.*

19. Ibid. For another interesting treatment and survey of the various first-century Jewish expectations about the Messiah and to see how they relate to the diverse aspects of Jesus' role as Messiah, see Jacob Neusner, William S. Green, and Ernest S. Frerichs, eds., *Judaisms and Their Messiahs at the Turn of the Christian Era* (New York: Cambridge University Press, 1987), 105, 231, 235, 241.

20. C. S. Lewis, *Christian Reflections* (Grand Rapids: Eerdmans, 1967), 10.

21. Baruch Moaz, *Priorities in Eschatology* (Rishon L'Tzion: Hagefen, 1991), 6, as quoted in Lisa Loden, "Differing Eschatological Viewpoints: Obstacles to Relationship?" *Mishkan*, 35 (2001): 4.

22. Arthur F. Glasser, "Eschatology and Christianity's Future in the Middle East," *Missionary Monthly,* April–May 1996, 11.

Chapter 3: The Way at the Well

1. Gary M. Burge, *Whose Land? Whose Promise? What Christians Are Not Being Told About Israel and the Palestinians* (Cleveland: Pilgrim, 2003), 81, 92.

2. Craig S. Keener, *IVP Bible Background Commentary: New Testament*, 2nd ed. (Downers Grove, IL: InterVarsity Press, 1994).

3. Ibid.

4. Ravi Zacharias, *Jesus Among Other Gods: The Absolute Claims of the Christian Message* (Nashville: W Publishing Group, 2000), 73.

5. For a similar instance in which Jesus made a clear self-disclosure of His messiahship and His deity to another broken and hurting person, see John 9.
6. See C. S. Lewis, *The Problem of Pain* (New York: Harper-Collins, 1996). See also Zacharias, *Jesus Among Other Gods*.
7. For a compelling discussion about the role God plays in the destinies of Hagar, Ishmael, and the Arabs, along with the Jews, see Tony Maalouf, *Arabs in the Shadow of Israel: The Unfolding of God's Prophetic Plan for Ishmael's Line* (Grand Rapids: Kregel, 2003).

Chapter 4: World Peace

1. *Miss Congeniality*, DVD, directed by Donald Petrie (2000; Burbank, CA: Warner Home Video, 2004).
2. See Gary R. Habermas and Michael R. Licona, *The Case for the Resurrection of Jesus* (Grand Rapids: Kregel, 2004), 67–69. The fact that Jesus' own brother James doubted Jesus' messiahship, as recorded in the Gospels does not detract from the authenticity of Jesus' mission. Rather, the opposite is true. First, that the Gospel writers Mark and John included this seemingly embarrassing fact shows the accuracy and authenticity of their accounts. Had the accounts been embellishments, surely the embarrassing fact that Jesus' own family, which included James, one of the pillars of the early Christian church, would have been left out or revised to show that Jesus' family was committed to following Him. Second, as we will later see, the fact that James was skeptical of Jesus' claims and later became the leader of the Jerusalem church actually shows that James's conversion was based on his sincere belief that he actually saw Jesus risen from the dead.
3. James Strong, *The Strongest Strong's Exhaustive Concordance of the Bible*, fully revised and corrected by John R.

Kohlenberger and James A. Swanson (Grand Rapids: Zondervan, 2001), 1462.

4. Ibid, 1493.

5. In fact, there are numerous early, extrabiblical accounts of the disciples' suffering and willingness to undergo it for the sake of the gospel of Jesus Christ, and His resurrection from the dead in particular. Clement of Rome (c. A.D. 30–100), Josephus (c. A.D. 37–100), Polycarp (c. A.D. 69–156), Ignatius (d. c. A.D. 107), Dionysius of Corinth (wrote c. A.D. 165–175), Origen (c. A.D. 185–254), Hegesippus (c. A.D. 110–180), Clement of Alexandria (c. A.D. 150–215), and Tertullian (c. A.D. 160–220) all wrote about the sufferings and martyrdoms of Jesus' early followers, particularly Peter, Paul, and James, Jesus' brother. Clement of Rome and Polycarp are especially significant because they personally knew the apostles Peter, John, and Paul. Josephus is also of particular significance because he was a non-Christian historian writing for the Roman Empire. For a detailed discussion of these ancient historical sources, see Habermas and Licona, *The Case for the Resurrection of Jesus*, 56–52nn. 46–66; 64–69nn. 12–25.

6. Ibid.

7. Eusebius, *Ecclesiastical History* 2.23; Flavius Josephus, *Antiquities* 20.200.

8. John Foxe, *Foxe's Book of Martyrs: A History of the Lives, Sufferings, and Deaths of the Early Christian and Protestant Martyrs*, ed. William Byron Forbush (Grand Rapids: Zondervan, 1967), 4.

9. Ravi Zacharias, *Can Man Live Without God* (New York: W Publishing Group, 1994), 157.

Chapter 5: The Crux of the Matter

1. Flavius Josephus, *The Wars of the Jews*, 2:5:1–3.

2. Many Muslims believe that Jesus was not crucified or killed but that it only appeared to the Jews and Romans

that He had been killed (Qur'an, Sura 4:156ff.). Muslims point to Jesus' requests for God to "take this cup" from Him as an indication that Jesus did not willingly go to the cross. Muslims believe that God granted Jesus' request and saved Him from death by making it appear that He had died when He did not, or by replacing Jesus with someone who was made to look like Jesus, perhaps Judas Iscariot or Simon of Cyrene. Of course, there is no historical evidence for either of these theories. In fact, the evidence is quite strong that Christ died on the cross and was seen as resurrected, as opposed to merely having survived the cross and the Roman scourging. See Gary Habermas, *The Risen Jesus and Future Hope* (Lanham, MD: Rowman and Littlefield, 1996). In addition, there are theological problems with these theories, which, in a very real sense, make God into a deceiver, not just of Jesus' enemies, but also of His closest followers, who went to their deaths preaching that Jesus died and rose from the dead.

3. John R. W. Stott, *The Cross of Christ* (Downers Grove, IL: InterVarsity Press, 2006), 76. In fact, Jesus did not shrink from this calling. The Gospels record that as Peter tried to violently protect Jesus from those who seized him, Jesus ordered Peter to stand down and allow His arrest. "Shall I not drink the cup which My Father has given Me?" He said to Peter (John 18:11).

4. Ibid., 77–78.

5. Ibid., 78. For additional references to the "cup" as a symbol of God's wrath, a symbol that would have been familiar to Jesus' contemporaries, see Job 21:20, Jeremiah 25:15–29, Ezekiel 23:32–34, and Isaiah 51:17–22.

6. Joachim Jeremias, *The Central Message of the New Testament* (Philadelphia: Fortress, 1965), 9–30; and Norman Perrin, *Rediscovering the Teaching of Jesus* (New York: Harper and Row, 1967), 37–41.

7. P. Barbet, *A Doctor at Calvary: The Passion of Our Lord Jesus Christ as Described by a Surgeon* (Garden City, NY:

Doubleday, 1953), 74–75; and William D. Edwards, Wesley J. Gabel, and Floyd E. Hosmer, "On the Physical Death of Jesus," *Journal of the American Medical Association* 255, no. 11 (March 21, 1986): 1456.

8. Stott, *The Cross of Christ*, 84.

9. Though Stott chooses not to accept this second explanation of why Jesus quoted Psalm 22, he grants that it is quite plausible. Ibid., 83.

10. Another way to view omnipotence is to hold that God is all-powerful in that He can cause any state of affairs, whether good or evil, but He does not cause an evil state of affairs because He is essentially good. On this view, God remains omnipotent in that He is *able* to do anything but does not do some things because in His essence He would not. In any case, God's nature is to be consistent and good, and so He is consistently good.

11. Kenneth Cragg, *Jesus and the Muslim* (Oxford: Oneworld Publications, 1999), 180–81.

12. Stott, *The Cross of Christ*, 90, quoting Anselm, *Cur Deus Homo?* trans. Edward S. Prout (London: Religious Tract Society, 1880), 1:21.

13. Ibid.

14. Ibid., 107.

15. R. W. Dale, *The Atonement* (London: Congregational Union of England and Wales, 1894), 338–39.

16. Stott, *The Cross of Christ*, 111.

17. For an excellent, detailed discussion of the Levitical laws regarding sacrifice and atonement, see Leon Morris, *The Atonement: Its Meaning and Significance* (Downers Grove, IL: InterVarsity Press, 1983).

18. Cragg, *Jesus and the Muslim*, 182.

19. For a further discussion of how Jesus' crucifixion logically satisfies the debts sinners have incurred, see Abdu Murray, "Jesus, Justification, and Justice" at http://www.4truth.net or http://www.embracethetruth.org.

20. Quoted in Martin H. Manser, *The Westminster Collection of Christian Quotations* (Louisville: Westminster John Knox Press, 2001), 112.

21. See 1 John 4:16.

22. It has been said that a concept's importance to a culture can be determined by how many words that culture has for the concept. For example, punctuality and efficiency are highly prized in the West, so we have numerous words just for timepieces (watch, clock, chronometer, chronograph, pocket watch, stopwatch, etc.). Arabs tend to value time much differently. We basically have one word in common parlance, *saa'ah*, that covers all of these concepts and even lumps other time-related concepts together. Family is very important to Arabs, however, so we have two words for uncle, two words for aunt, and at least four words just to describe our first cousins.

23. See Ravi Zacharias, *Can Man Live Without God* (New York: W Publishing Group, 1994), 148–50.

24. C. S. Lewis, *Mere Christianity* (New York: Macmillan, 1952), 120.

25. Isaac Watts, *Hymns and Spiritual Songs*, 1707, emphasis added.

26. G. K. Chesterton, *Orthodoxy* (New York: Doubleday, 2001), 168–70.

Chapter 6: Ripples and Reflections

1. *The Humanist Manifesto III* can be viewed in its entirety at http://www.americanhumanist.org/3/Humanismandits Aspirations.pdf.

2. See e.g., Qur'an, *Al-Maidah* 5:9; *Al-Anfal* 8:29; *Ash-Shura* 2:26. I am, of course, well aware that the Qur'an teaches that God is "oft forgiving, most merciful," but it is equally true that God's forgiveness and mercy is tied to whether a person does good works, as the contexts of the Qur'anic verses cited above show.

3. Philip Yancey, *Soul Survivor: How Thirteen Unlikely Mentors Helped My Faith Survive the Church* (New York: Doubleday, 2001), 58.
4. Ibid.
5. Ibid.
6. Some have attributed this statement to C. S. Lewis, but I have been unable to conclusively determine its source.

Chapter 7: And Now These Three Remain

1. Avid college basketball fans will recall the University of Michigan's famous "Fab Five," which included Chris Webber, Jalen Rose, Juwan Howard, Jimmy King, and Ray Jackson, all of whom were top college basketball prospects and all of whom were entering college the same time I was.
2. My closest friend and brother in Christ, Mickey Badalamenti, gave this sermon. I am forever grateful that I was present to hear his teaching firsthand. I summarize his sermon here with his permission.
3. Gershom Scholem, "Toward an Understanding of the Messianic Idea in Judaism," in *The Messianic Idea in Judaism* (New York: Schoken, 1971), 1; quoted by William S. Green, "Messiah in Judaism: Rethinking the Question," in *Judaisms and Their Messiahs at the Turn of the Christian Era*, ed. Jacob Neusner, William S. Green, and Ernest Fredrichs (New York: Cambridge University Press, 1987), 9–10.
4. See Stanley Weintraub, *Silent Night: The Story of the World War I Christmas Truce* (New York: Free Press, 2001).